THE DAILY ENTREPRENUER

33 Success Habits for Small Business Owners, Freelancers and Aspiring 9-to-5 Escape Artists

By Steve "S.J." Scott

www.HabitBooks.com

&

Rebecca Livermore

www.ProfessionalContentCreation.com

ISBN: 1503014517
ISBN-13: 978-1503014510

Disclaimer

4

Table of Contents

Your Two Free Gifts

As a way of saying *thanks* for your purchase, we're offering two free report that are exclusive to our book and blog readers. First up is Rebecca's eCourse, *The Five Secrets to Developing the Blogging Habit.*

To get your complimentary eCourse delivered right to your inbox, go to http://professionalcontentcreation.com/blogginghabit

Next, in Steve's book *77 Good Habits to Live a Better Life,* you'll discover a variety of routines that can help you in many different areas of your life. You will learn how to make lasting changes to your work, success, learning, health and sleep habits.

This lengthy PDF (over 12,000 words) reviews each habit and provides a simple action plan. Check out this link: http://www.developgoodhabits.com/FREE

Introduction

Entrepreneurship is exciting, but it can also be stressful, frustrating and overwhelming.

You may have started your entrepreneurial journey with a rosy idea of what it would be like to finally stop working for someone else, but the reality is that success is often harder to come by on your own.

For instance, a regular job has a schedule, with severe consequences for not showing up when you're supposed to. Bosses tell you what to do, and coworkers are there to confer with when you get stuck. Best of all, problems (like when a computer system goes down) aren't actually your problem when you work for someone else. If *someone else* owns it, they are responsible for fixing it.

The freedom you have as an entrepreneur is a definite perk, but it can also be a heavy burden, especially when you lack motivation or encounter a problem that you don't know how to solve.

Perhaps your business isn't growing as much as you'd like. Maybe your bank account balance doesn't match up with the long hours you work. There may even be times when you feel forced to make things up as you go along.

The good news is, the problems you face are common and experienced by most—if not all—entrepreneurs. In fact, if you study the lives of successful people, you'll find that, regardless of industry, they faced the same challenges you face and found a way to overcome them.

When you look closely at the lives of successful entrepreneurs, you'll find that **the secret to their success was developing good habits**.

For example, Jerry Seinfeld didn't become funny overnight. He developed his joke-telling ability by practicing the habit of writing a joke every single day.

In *On Writing, A Memoir of the Craft* (http://www.amazon.com/On-Writing-Anniversary-Edition-Memoir/dp/1439156816), Stephen King recommends sticking to a strict writing schedule. He has a habit of writing ten pages per day, six to seven days per week, including holidays.

Kobe Bryant is known for practicing basketball—a lot. He doesn't just practice; he practices with purpose. Before each session, Bryant develops a plan (such as shooting 800 jump shots) with the goal of improving one specific skill.

As you can see from the examples above, the focus isn't on working long hours (although long hours may be necessary at times). The point here is that habitually focusing on the important things will often lead to success.

Successful entrepreneurs aren't always the ones with the most talent. They face many of the same challenges you and I face. What sets them apart is their solid foundation of habits and daily routines.

In the following book, *The Daily Entrepreneur: 33 Success Habits for Small Business Owners, Freelancers and Aspiring 9-to-5 Escape Artists*, we talk about the power of habit development and explain how to use it to overcome the challenges you face on a regular basis as an entrepreneur.

What makes this book different is that it is organized according to specific business challenges. We outline the strategies and habits you need to develop to overcome these obstacles. Finally, each habit comes with a simple action plan for implementing the information.

Who Are We?

Steve (or "S.J.") runs the blog *Develop Good Habits* (http://www.developgoodhabits.com/). The goal of his site is to show how *continuous* habit development can lead to a better life. Instead of lecturing you, he provides simple strategies you can start using right away. His goal is to show how you can make lasting changes by developing one quality habit at a time.

Steve has been a successful online entrepreneur for more than a decade, running websites that cover a variety of niches and income strategies. He's learned a number of things in these last 10 years, especially how important it is to focus on what's *actually* working and make sure your business model is constantly evolving.

Rebecca is the owner of *Professional Content Creation* (http://professionalcontentcreation.com/), and a freelance writer and content strategy consultant for small businesses. She's been privileged to work with some of the top names in content marketing and social media such as Michael Hyatt, Amy Porterfield, Marcus Sheridan and Pat Flynn. Many of the success habits that have become part of her life and business have come about as a result of learning from and modeling the behavior of some of her most successful clients.

Rebecca is a creative and naturally disorganized person. She was always known as someone who did a great job organizing things on paper—only to lose the piece of paper. This changed once she developed good systems for keeping track of all of her tasks and ideas.

She knows what it means to do the sidehustle because she started her business while working full time. She's now been working at home full time, without a boss to oversee her efforts, for three years. During that time, she's gone from working far too many hours for too little pay to taking control of her time and getting the most important things done by early afternoon. This change occurred as she learned the power of developing habits and running her business according to a plan rather than living in a constant state of emergency.

As you can see, this book is a collaborative effort between Steve and Rebecca. We both provide bits of knowledge from our personal experiences, plus we've talked to a number of entrepreneurs who also share their thoughts.

Another thing you might have noticed is that, when providing anecdotes, we use the third person tense (e.g., "Steve remembers…" or "Rebecca's friend…"). This was intentionally done to make it easier for you to follow the narrative of the book. We'll admit that it's a bit clunky, but you'll find it's easier to grasp the information if you know who is telling the story.

Who Is This Book For?

If you're a part-time or full-time entrepreneur, this book is for you. For the purpose of all being on the same page, we define an entrepreneur as anyone who:

- Does freelance work
- Runs a business (both online and offline)
- Is self-employed in any way
- Wants to create a side income or is interested in a sidehustle
- Is creative and wants to sell their craft (e.g., artists, musicians and writers)

Bottom line: If you have a passion for generating an income outside of a traditional nine to five setting, then this is the book for you.

5 Challenges Entrepreneurs Experience

Finally, we were very deliberate when picking the format of this book. Instead of simply listing 33 habits in no particular order, we identified the five biggest challenges entrepreneurs face (regardless of industry) and then described specific habits to overcome them:

1. Failing to achieve professional goals
2. Not getting things done
3. Increasing competition
4. Poor business relationships
5. Stress and burnout

You'll find it's easier to understand the "why" behind each habit when you see how it directly relates to a challenge you regularly experience. First we'll start with the basics of habit development and how to implement these success habits into your daily routine. Then the rest of the book is broken down into these five major sections, each profiling what we call "Entrepreneur Success Habits" or ESH for short.

There's a lot to cover, so let's jump in and talk about the importance of forming positive habits.

9 Steps for Developing a New Habit

As you will see, many entrepreneurial habits are included in this book. Some only take a few minutes of time, others require a total overhaul of your routine and a few can be done once per week.

It would be a mistake to try them all at once. The smarter strategy is to focus on your biggest current challenge and form habits to overcome it.

So, how do you develop a new habit?

In this section, we provide a quick crash course on habit development, which you can use to add positive routines to your entrepreneurial day.

Why Motivation Doesn't Work

We've all done this before. You start a new habit excited about what you'll accomplish. You do it for a few days; then something unexpected happens, so you skip a day. Suddenly the habit becomes challenging. You've lost that desire to keep going, so you miss another day or two. Finally, you quit because you feel a "lack of motivation" to keep going.

The truth is motivation is a myth when it comes to habit development. You can't always rely on desire alone to continue a routine. Your efforts will fail the first time you're busy or not feeling well. Instead, you need to take action—even when you're not in the mood.

Steve runs and writes on a regular basis. Often he doesn't feel "motivated" to do either activity. Yet he does both simply because they're part of his long-term goals and *identity* (more on this later).

You'll discover the same thing with the following entrepreneur habits. At times, you won't feel like doing one of them. These are the moments when it's important to take action simply because it's an established routine—like showering, eating and brushing your teeth.

To help you get started, I recommend this brief nine-step plan for turning an action into a regular habit.

Step 1: Focus on One Habit at a Time

Steve has studied a lot about habit development and implemented many habits in his life. His one piece of advice is to focus on changing only one habit at a time. The reason relates to something known as "ego depletion," which is covered extensively in the book *Willpower* (http://www.developgoodhabits.com/willpower) by Roy F. Baumeister and John Tierney.

In that book, the authors define ego depletion as "a person's diminished capacity to regulate their thoughts, feelings and actions."

The basic premise is that willpower is like a muscle that weakens as it's used throughout the day. We don't have a limitless supply of willpower; once we've used up our supply for the day, it's gone. At that point, it becomes very hard to exercise discipline.

Ego depletion impacts our ability to form new habits because our supply of willpower is spread out among all areas of our lives. Because of this, it's important to work on only one habit at a time. That way, your store of willpower can be channeled into completing that one habit, increasing the odds of success.

The best practice is to pick and choose the habits from this book that best fit your personal situation, in any order that makes the most sense to you. Try focusing on one habit until you've turned it into an automatic action.

Step 2: Build a Habit-Stacking Routine (Optional)

There is an exception to the rule outlined above. It's possible to develop multiple habits at once. The trick here to make sure that each habit is too small to fail—only requiring a few minutes to complete. Instead of scattering them throughout the day, you string them together into a step-by-step routine Steve calls "habit stacking."

The idea behind habit stacking is simple—you identify a habit you've already established, like getting out of bed every morning, and use it as a trigger to start the routine. Then you complete a series of quick (no more than five minutes each) habits in a pre-determined sequence. What goes into this sequence is up to you. It could include *only* entrepreneurial habits or it could be a mix from the different areas of your life.

As an example, every morning Steve completes a habit-stacking routine that includes reviewing his goals, drinking a high-energy smoothie, texting his fiancée a loving message, completing a five-minute mediation session and recording the completion of specific habits in Lift.do.

Each is important for a different reason. By putting them into a single routine, Steve doesn't need to rely on six different triggers to complete six different actions. He simply follows the checklist for one habit-stacking routine.

As an entrepreneur, you can start the workday with a habit stack. Here's an example:

- Identify your top priorities.
- Review your goals.
- Scan advertising campaigns.
- Create one new test campaign.
- Review what you learned from the previous day.
- Reach out to one person in your industry.
- Organize your immediate work environment.

The beauty of habit stacking is you can easily turn a 15- to 30 -minute block of time into a powerful routine that sets the stage for a very productive day.

Step #3: Commit to the Habit for 30 Days

Some people say it takes 21 days to build a habit, while others claim it takes up to 66 days. The truth is the length of time really varies. You'll find that some habits are easy to build, while others require more effort. My advice is to commit to a single habit for the next 30 days (or a month to keep it simple). During this time, your entire life should be structured around the completion of this one action.

Why 30 days?

It's simple. Steve likes the symmetry of a month-long habit as a way to "test drive" a new behavior. Let's face it; some habits aren't fun to do on a regular basis. However, it's easy to do something unpleasant if you're only committing for a month. When the time expires, you can either decide to continue with the habit or simply start a new one.

What's really great about a 30-day commitment is you get confidence. You get to know what it's like to follow a habit on a day-to-day basis. You understand both the positive and negative triggers—the things that ultimately determine whether you complete a habit on a daily basis. This information becomes invaluable when you work to improve your new ritual.

It's hard to pinpoint how long it'll take to build a new habit, but commit to it for the next 30 days and you'll quickly see if it helps your business.

Step #4: Anchor the New Habit to an Established Habit

B.J. Fogg has done extensive research into habit development with his course Tiny Habits (http://tinyhabits.com/). The premise here is to commit to a very small habit change and take baby steps as you build on it. An important aspect of his teachings is to "anchor" the new habit to something you already do on a daily basis.

The example he uses is to create a habit using this recipe:

"After I [your anchor], I will [new habit]."

When you pick a new habit, start by identifying a routine that you reliably do on a daily basis. Then attach the new habit to this behavior.

Here are a few examples:

- "After I sit at my desk in the morning, I will write down my top three priorities for the day."
- "After I walk into my home, I will put my keys and wallet/purse on my nightstand."
- "After I stop work for the day, I will mentally review the one lesson I learned during the day."

Think carefully about all the automatic actions you take on a daily basis. Odds are, you'll discover lots of pre-established routines. Simply take your new habit and anchor it to one of these actions.

Step #5: Take Baby Steps

Think back to our brief discussion of motivation. The danger of relying on motivation alone is you don't have a backup plan when you're not in the mood. Really, the only way to make a habit stick is to turn it into automatic behavior. You can do this by taking baby steps and creating a low level of commitment.

As an example, writing is a huge part of Steve and Rebecca's businesses. While they both consistently write 1,000+ words per day, it would be silly for you to immediately start with that goal. Instead, it would be better to commit to a small goal like writing 100 words or even a single sentence.

The idea here is to create a micro-commitment where it's impossible to fail. It's more important to stay consistent and not miss a day than it is to hit a specific milestone. What you'll find is that when you have a low level of commitment, you'll be more likely to get started.

With a new habit, create a goal that's too small to fail. Stay focused on what you need to do right now and ignore future milestones. Then make tiny, incremental changes. At first, you won't notice a shift in your habits. However, on a long enough timeline, you'll develop a permanent change to your routine.

Step #6: Create Accountability for the New Habit

Track your day-to-day habit change and make public declarations about your new routine. According to the Hawthorne Effect (http://www.developgoodhabits.com/hawthorne-effect/), you're more likely to follow through with a commitment when you're being observed by others. So to stick with this new routine, you should let others know about your efforts.

Post updates on social media accounts, use apps like Chains (https://chains.cc/) & Lift (http://lift.do/) to track your progress, work with an accountability partner or post regular updates on an online community related to the habit. Do whatever it takes to get reinforcement from others about this new routine.

Never underestimate the power of social approval. Simply *knowing* you will be held accountable for your habit keeps you focused and consistent.

Step #7: Overcome Setbacks with an If-Then Plan

It's easy to slip and miss a day. What you can't afford to do is turn this one mistake into a snowball where you stop trying and ultimately give up.

One solution is to plan for these setbacks and know what you'll do when they occur. Start by writing down the obstacles that often get in your way. Your list might include feeling unmotivated, being distracted by technology or experiencing unexpected work emergencies.

After that, create a strategy for how you'll handle these challenges (this is often called "if-then planning"). The point here is to fully understand how you typically fail and learn what to do when a specific scenario comes up.

For instance, let's say you have trouble with working on priority projects during the first part of the day. You could create a series of if-then plans that deal with the challenges that you face on a regular basis:

- "If I get distracted in the morning by family members, then I will wake up earlier and work on priority tasks before everyone else gets up."
- "If my inbox becomes distracting, then I will commit to not checking until 10 a.m. every day."
- "If I find myself working on urgent (but not important) tasks in the morning, then I will start each day with a list of important tasks and do these before anything else."

You'll find that no habit is perfect when you first start it. It usually takes some experimentation before you settle on a routine you can complete on a regular basis.

Step #8: Reward Important Milestones

Building habits doesn't have to be boring. Instead, you want to build a reward system into the process so you celebrate the successful creation of an entrepreneurial habit. What you pick is up to you, but it's important to celebrate those big moments in the life of your business.

Furthermore, a reward doesn't have to break the bank. You could check out a new movie, enjoy a night out with your significant other, take a day off from your hard work or simply do something that you love.

We often underestimate the importance of having "fun" while building habits. Often, though, having a clear reward for regularly completing an action will help you to stick to the new routine.

Step #9: Build a New Identity

Repeating a habit on a daily basis will only get you so far. You can do a lot by committing to a small action, doing it every day, increasing the effort over time and overcoming obstacles. But at some point, you need to go from simply doing it every day to making it part of your core identity. Only then will you stick to it without the constant need for reinforcement.

James Clear often talks about something he calls Identity-Based Habits (http://jamesclear.com/identity-based-habits). The idea here is you can build a lasting habit by making it a reflection of who you are on the inside. Simply put, you need to believe the habit is part of what makes YOU a unique person.

He emphasizes the fact that most goals (and habits) are centered on a specific outcome (like generating a specific level of income or winning industry-specific accolades).

It's better to decide that the habit is simply part of your identity and then use each "small win" as a way to demonstrate that it's who you are on the inside.

Really, it starts with a shift of mindset. With a new habit, reinforce this behavior by saying things like: "I'm the type of person who _____." Then, follow through by doing it on a daily basis. Eventually your internal identity will match this daily routine.

As an example, Steve is most proud of two identity-based habits—running and writing.

Let's face it. Both can be boring to do on a daily basis. Yet he's able to consistently complete these habits, simply because he identifies himself as both a runner and a writer.

When Steve feels a lack of motivation, he still completes these habits because he knows that not doing them wouldn't match the identity he's built about himself.

You'll find that forming an identity around a habit is the "secret sauce" to making it stick. When an action becomes part of who you are, often you'll do it simply because it's as natural as eating or brushing your teeth.

Well, you now have a quick action plan for building new habits. Let's jump into the meat of this book and start with the first challenge entrepreneurs regularly experience.

Challenge #1: Failing To Achieve Professional Goals

Starting a business is one thing, but making it profitable for the long haul is quite another.

Though exact numbers are hard to come by, many experts believe 50 percent of all businesses fail in the first year. The numbers are even more discouraging in the years that follow, with 90 to 95 percent of all businesses failing in the first five years.

While it's true that a poor economy can be a contributing factor in the failure of a business, in many cases failure is a direct result of an entrepreneur's inability to take specific actions that drive the business forward.

In order to beat the odds, you must develop a "success at all costs" attitude that separates winners from losers. Even with a great attitude, without the right habits, you may find yourself working hard with little to show for it.

In this section we'll talk about the challenge of not achieving your professional goals. To overcome this obstacle, you need to focus on building these five habits:

- ESH #1: Start with a market need
- ESH #2: Embrace failure
- ESH #3: Identify hidden opportunities
- ESH #4: Provide value to customers
- ESH #5: Wake up early

Not hitting your professional and financial goals is the first sign of a business that's about to fail, so pay close attention to these habits to learn how to turn things around.

ESH #1: Start with a Market Need

Many entrepreneurs start their businesses based on passion rather than reason. While passion helps you stick with a business for the long haul, market demand will ultimately determine your success.

Doing market research is the best way to determine if your "great idea" truly is a great idea. It's best to do this *before* you spend a ton of time and money launching the new product or service.

The good news is, if the market research does uncover a true need, then all you have to do is come up with a great solution, find a way to tap into the market and then deliver your solution.

Rebecca's friend, author Nina Amir (http://ninaamir.com/), finds that blogging about her books helps her find out what does and doesn't resonate with her audience. She then makes adjustments based on this feedback before publishing each title.

Steve spent weeks researching the "habits" niche before publishing books. He researched countless websites, blogs and podcasts to see if people were interested in this topic. Then he closely examined the existing content on the Kindle platform to see if there was a "hole in the marketplace." Only when he was sure that the idea had profit potential did he start his website, DevelopGoodHabits.com.

At a mall near Rebecca, there is a company that asks shoppers to give their opinions in exchange for a small monetary reward. Participants are asked for their opinions on everything from advertising campaigns to products and pricing. These factors ultimately determine whether or not a product should be released and, if so, what pricing strategies/advertising campaigns are most likely to succeed.

While you probably don't have the means to rent space in a mall, hire a team of surveyors or pay incentives to survey participants, you can conduct similar types of research. Simply survey your email list subscribers, poll your blog readers, have face-to-face conversations with customers and talk to people who might want to buy your potential solution.

To illustrate this point, Rebecca has an autoresponder email with the subject line, *"I need your help."*

Here she asks subscribers to talk about their biggest problems with content marketing. In exchange for their responses, she replies to the emails personally and answers every question. Rebecca then uses this information to write blog posts and develop products. When she finds that multiple people have the same problem, she knows she's onto something.

Another way to start with a market need is to create what's called a "minimum viable product" (MVP), then release it to a small test group to measure the overall response.

For instance, you could write a low-cost Kindle book before creating a full-blown information product. If readers like it, then you know the idea is worth your time and money.

The bottom line is that one of the best habits you can develop as an entrepreneur is one of listening to the people in your target audience to discover the types of solutions they need.

IMPLEMENTATION

Here are four actions for starting with a market need.

Action 1: Rather than creating content for your website haphazardly, plan your content around ideas you want to test out. Blog content is not only a great way to build an audience, but also useful for measuring how people respond to an idea.

You should also do these two things on a weekly basis: 1. Check your Google Analytics to see what content gets the most views. 2. Spy on your competition using the tool BuzzSumo (http://buzzsumo.com/). Enter keywords related to your business and see what topics get the biggest buzz on social media.

Action 2: Get into the habit of testing everything you do (subject lines for emails, opt-in forms, package designs, pricing, etc.).

Action 3: Run regular ads targeting your primary customer. Make note of which potential products your audience members seem interested in.

Action 4: When talking to customers on a one-on-one level, ask about the challenges they regularly experience. Find out what type of solution would make a measurable difference in their lives.

ESH #2: Embrace Failure

Odds are you're reading this book because you want your business to succeed. Nobody sets out to fail. But whether you like it or not, failure can be an important stepping-stone on the road to success. In fact, it can often catapult you to success!

The key here is to understand that everyone experiences failure. You are not a failure simply because something you tried didn't work out.

The difference between those who ultimately succeed and those who quit are that successful entrepreneurs view failure as a learning opportunity. As Henry Ford famously quoted, "Failure is simply the opportunity to begin again, this time more intelligently."

Ford wasn't just being witty when he said that. His first car company failed, and he certainly isn't alone in his experience. Steve Jobs was fired from Apple, and yet when he was brought back on, he completely turned the company around and transformed it into the much-loved brand it is today.

You've no doubt heard about Edison's failed attempts when it came to inventing a filament that would make incandescent light bulbs viable. There are many different versions of the story that vary his number of attempts from 700 to 1,000 to 10,000.

Regardless of the exact number of attempts, the bottom line is that it took a lot of tries to get it right. Even more important than Edison's sheer tenacity was the attitude that fueled his tenacity. In fact, he didn't see what we would call failed attempts as failures. Instead, he saw them as successes because they allowed him to discover what didn't work. He recognized that the only way to figure out what would work was by first discovering what didn't work.

The key with Edison—and every other person who has achieved massive success—is that, after failing, he got back up and took action.

Another key is that successful entrepreneurs aren't afraid to try, even when the odds of success are slim. For instance, when

Michael Hyatt advertised that he was looking for a podcast producer, Rebecca applied for the position, even though her podcasting experience was pretty limited at the time.

She somehow miraculously made it into the final three and was interviewed over the phone by Michael. In the end, another candidate was selected for the position.

While Rebecca was a bit disappointed, she used this experience to motivate her to improve her podcasting skills. She started her own podcast and took additional podcasting training. She went on to provide podcast production support for other big-name people and now works as a podcast consultant.

Even more amazing is that her failed attempt to become Michael Hyatt's podcast producer made Michael and his team aware of her talents. When they needed a content manager and were writing the job description, they immediately thought of Rebecca and ended up offering her the job.

It's human nature to want to lick your wounds when you fail. And it's okay to do that—up to a point. You have to get up and try again—and again if needed—to experience true success.

Criticism Is Failure's Younger Sibling

While criticism isn't as severe as out and out failure, it's still an indication that someone wasn't quite pleased, and it stings. Criticism can wound an ego and make you want to quit.

Rebecca has worked for some very successful people and a common trait among them is their insistence on excellence. The level of work that was acceptable for most of her earlier clients was deemed not good enough by others. Her early attempts at work for these clients were often sent back, and sometimes she had to redo things multiple times before they were approved. These experiences bruised her ego because she was used to being praised. She had to learn that the feedback she received wasn't a personal attack.

Steve regularly receives criticism on his books—some is helpful and some not so helpful. The important mindset he has is to view each negative review as an opportunity to find out what his readers want and then to use this information to improve the quality of the next book.

The Benefits of Failure and Criticism

Regardless of whether you experience true failure or simply have your work criticized as we have, there are four benefits to receiving this small taste of negative feedback:

Benefit 1: Develop a standard of excellence. In Rebecca's case, working for people with a high standard of excellence has improved the overall quality of her work and enabled her to stand out as one of the best in her industry.

Benefit 2: You'll get feedback about what people actually think about your product. We dream about people praising our products, but criticism helps you learn up front—before spending too much time and money—what people really think about your product.

Benefit 3: You'll have an edge over your competitors. Chances are, your competitors face many of the same challenges you encounter. If you find a solution and they don't, this will put you miles ahead of them.

Benefit 4: You'll get empirical evidence about the results of a tested strategy. This may force you to try a new direction that you didn't originally consider.

Bottom line: When you take action after a failure, you'll develop a subconscious ability to know how to regularly overcome adversity. Ultimately, this habit will give you a competitive advantage over the people who allow one small hiccup to derail their entire business.

IMPLEMENTATION

Failure happens all the time. You can quickly overcome this challenge by doing the following:

Action 1: Try something new on a weekly—if not daily—basis, even if you think the odds of success are slim.

Action 2: Start a file with stories of people who have first failed and then later succeeded. They can be stories about famous people such as Thomas Edison and his light bulb or everyday people such as Rebecca and the failure that eventually led her to success with Michael Hyatt.

Don't forget to add your own stories to this file. In times of failure or doubt, review the stories for a good shot of motivation.

Action 3: On a daily basis, affirm that failure is part of the process. For instance, you may want to use something like Edison's "I have not failed, I've just found 10,000 ways that won't work."

This ongoing affirmation is important because, even if you accept the need to embrace failure on an intellectual level, it's still normal to feel upset when you fail.

Action 4: On a daily basis, ask yourself, "What is one thing that didn't go according to plan?" Consider what you can learn from it.

Action 5: Network with other entrepreneurs and find out what they've done to overcome similar problems. Both Steve and Rebecca are in mastermind groups where they can safely discuss challenges and victories in their businesses.

If you have the funds, work with a coach or mentor to find out what they've done to overcome similar problems.

Action 6: Follow the example of most successful people who take a tactical approach to building their businesses. That approach looks something like this:

- A. Set an initial goal.
- B. Take a small step toward that goal, such as using paid advertising to test a market and see if there are actual customers willing to pay for the product.
- C. Learn from that action and see what you could have done differently.

D. Apply this lesson by taking another step.
E. Keep building and learning along the way.

ESH #3: Identify Hidden Opportunities

Unexpected change can seem catastrophic, especially when the change occurs against your will. But sometimes so-called disasters are filled with opportunities that wouldn't be there (or be noticed) had the seemingly negative situation not occurred.

Rebecca recently went through a big change in her business that resulted in the loss of about 75 percent of her income. This was a scary thing, and might be considered disastrous by many, but the change in business freed up time to do things that would have otherwise been very difficult, if not impossible, to manage with her previous workload. In a sense, she had to walk away from something many people considered good in order to do something better.

Change, even when it seems disastrous, provides incredible opportunities if you're able to look at seeming disasters through the lens of possibility.

Now granted, this is easier said than done, especially when the sting of the disaster is still fresh. The good news is that it's okay to initially be upset when disaster strikes. But don't let yourself stay in a state of fear, anger or depression. Instead, train yourself to look at the positive aspects of a disaster to see how your business can potentially benefit from what you've learned.

For example, Rebecca realized that, had her situation not become painful, she would have stayed put even though many aspects of the work caused her a lot of stress. Things had to become bad in order for her to embrace the good. Hitting a crisis point was necessary for her ultimate fulfillment.

Disasters not only push you out of your comfort zone, they also make you evaluate your priorities. The key is to look at what the disaster makes possible, and then go for it wholeheartedly.

IMPLEMENTATION

You'd be surprised at how many opportunities arise from seemingly disastrous situations. The important step is to take the time to carefully analyze past challenges and use them to gain perspective on current events when you feel stressed. Here are few ideas for getting started:

Action 1: If you tend toward pessimism, it will be more difficult for you to see opportunities in the face of disaster. Therefore, train yourself to see the good by regularly evaluating your day or week, making note of what went wrong and jotting down ideas (both small and large) about the good that could come as a result of the bad.

Action 2: Think about the difficulties you've had in the past, whether in your personal or professional life, and make note of good things that occurred in your life as a result of each disaster.

Action 3: To prime the pump, open up a journal or Word doc and come up with as many items as possible for the following prompt: *"If [this bad thing] hadn't happened, [this good thing] would not have occurred."*

Action 4: Pick three areas of your life and think about the worst things that could possibly happen in those areas. Then think about what you would do if your worst-case scenarios came true. For example, you might think about what you would do if you lost a big client, lost your home or lost some aspect of your health.

Action 5: Develop a solid contingency plan regarding potential disasters in your business.

As an example, Steve's income relies heavily on the Amazon platform. However, he understands the inherent risk of being too reliant on one stream of income, so he's done a few things to minimize the damage in case catastrophe strikes:

1. He's saved a substantial portion of his royalties, creating an emergency fund.
2. He has reinvested some money into other income-generating side projects.
3. He has a game plan for making a successful pivot in case Amazon makes a sudden rule change.

The point with all of these actions is to develop the habit of optimism. Sometimes bad things happen, but if you look closely, you'll discover a few hidden opportunities that might not be apparent to other entrepreneurs.

ESH #4: Provide Value to Customers

We've all had times when we're delighted by a company's customer service. Other times we're appalled by a poor experience. However, most of our customer service experiences are somewhere in the middle—not memorable in any way.

Your goal as an entrepreneur should be to be unforgettable—for positive reasons, of course. One way to consistently provide value is to be in the habit of looking for ways to give a little extra attention, even when you're not expected to do so.

Recently Rebecca asked some of her friends to share their stories about providing value to customers. Use the following to get the wheels turning and find ways to do a little extra for your customers.

Jim shared, "I went to a Mexican restaurant for lunch. It's one of those places where you go through the line and they prepare your food per your specifications. When I got to the register and reached for my wallet, I realized I had left it at home. I apologized and told the cashier that I could go home and get my wallet. The cashier told me not to worry about it; the meal was on them. I now make a point of eating there regularly—always being sure to remember my wallet!"

Elizabeth shared, "A brand new grocery store had just opened, and I called to make sure they had fresh thyme. The produce guy assured me they did. I was shopping for Thanksgiving and had small children. I wanted to make sure I could purchase all my ingredients in one stop. I went to the store I'd called and loaded my cart with all the fixings for a delicious turkey dinner.

When I arrived in the produce section, there was no thyme! I wasn't going to complain, but when the checker asked, "Did you find everything you needed?" I told her what had happened. She alerted the produce manager, who apologized profusely. He then wrote down my address and drove across town to another store in their chain for a bunch of fresh thyme.

He delivered it to my door within a half hour. He wouldn't even let me pay for the herbs. That one well-executed act of customer service launched a relationship with that store that lasted 10 years—until we moved from the community!"

Joan shared, "One of my favorite companies is the Comfort Company, a company that deals with loss. They have fabulous treasures and ship them very quickly and at no charge. I purchased an ornament for a friend who lost her mother. The way my friend described the ornament on Facebook, I was concerned that they may have shipped the wrong one. I called the company to check on this, and they not only looked into it, but actually called my friend to make sure she had received the proper ornament. They then called me back to let me know all was well. I always get excellent service from this company, and their products are reasonably priced."

CelebriDucks (http://celebriducks.com/) has had great success in an unlikely niche—rubber ducks. They have an entire line of celebrity ducks and have been voted one of the top 100 gifts by *Entertainment Weekly* and featured on media outlets such as *The Tonight Show*.

To keep from becoming static or stale, they continually offer new rubber ducks while retiring other ducks. They brought the entire rubber duck industry back to America, where it originated. What sets them apart is providing a large variety of rubber ducks not offered elsewhere.

The key in all of these stories is doing more than is expected, and in many cases doing it without the customer having to ask. It's worth going out of your way to provide exceptional value and create experiences for your customers that they will never forget.

IMPLEMENTATION

Providing value to customers can be habitualized in a number of ways. It comes down to creating a great process and positively engaging with customers on a daily basis. Here are a few strategies to get started:

Action 1: Think carefully about ongoing problems and projects. What has been a success and what has been a failure? Consider how you can make improvements, even if your current offerings are considered "good enough."

Do this *at least* once a month, and look for ways to systematize procedures to reduce the number of times mistakes happen.

Action 2: If something does get missed or a mistake is made, take full responsibility. Review the error, learn lessons from it and use this misstep to make improvements to your overall process.

Develop the daily practice of reviewing each customer interaction. Do your best to solve their immediate problems, but also write down ideas on how you could have prevented the situation in the first place. Then take corrective action so you can immediately apply what you've learned to your business.

Action 3: Take action early, before issues arise, even if you think customers won't complain about something that is subpar. Always be on the lookout for ways to go the extra mile and do the unexpected for your customers.

For instance, Steve makes a point of putting more depth and substance into every book he writes, without raising his prices. Also, some readers have told him he should provide more examples from other people. As you can see from this book, he is following this suggestion by including a lot of anecdotes from other entrepreneurs.

Action 4: Look at what your competitors do and make a point of doing a better job or offering something they don't provide. The essence of this idea is to look for "holes in the marketplace." When you identify a major problem and then provide a great solution, customers will be more likely to do business with your company.

You can easily turn this last action into a monthly habit. Block out an hour or so on the first day of each month to do competitive analysis. Identify your top few competitors and study their offerings.

Ask yourself: *What are the positive things their customers have to say? How about the negative? What mistakes are they making? Are they not fulfilling a specific demand? What can I do to improve on their success?*

ESH #5: Wake Up Early

Morning is the most important part of your workday—even if you're not a morning person.

Most successful entrepreneurs wake up as much as three hours earlier than their unsuccessful counterparts.

Recently, Rebecca read an article titled *29 Successful People Who Wake Up Really Early* (http://www.businessinsider.com/successful-people-who-wake-up-really-early-2013-12?op=1). You can get an idea of what it takes to succeed by observing what these individuals do to start their days:

- Brooklyn Nets CEO Brett Yormark is up at 3:30 so that he can make it to his office by 4:30. Once there, he works out and sends motivational emails to his team.
- General Motors CEO Dan Akerson rarely wakes up later than 4:30 or 5:00. Working during the early morning hours makes it possible for him to connect with his associates in Asia before it's too late.
- Hain Celestial Group CEO Irwin Simon is up by 5:00 a.m. He spends his early morning hours going through emails, checking on operations in Europe and Asia, praying, walking his dog and exercising before his kids get up.
- Square CEO Jack Dorsey rises at 5:30, which gives him the time he needs to meditate and run six miles before starting his workday.
- Richard Branson, founder and chairman of the Virgin Group, is up by 5:45 a.m. and spends the first part of his day exercising and having an early breakfast before heading into work.

As you can see from the above examples, these successful entrepreneurs start their days between 3:30 and 5:30 a.m. and use their early morning hours to do the following:

- Catch up on email
- Pray/meditate
- Exercise
- Read
- Catch up on news
- Take care of family members (including pets) before heading into the office
- Eat breakfast
- Connect with people in different time zones

We all have our personal preferences regarding the most "important" way to start the day. For instance, Steve often strongly discourages people from starting the day by going through their inboxes, but that's what many top-level CEOs do first thing in the morning. The key here is to focus on the activity that has the biggest impact on your business (more on this later).

Still not sure if waking up early is right for you?

Well, here are four benefits of developing the "wake up early" habit:

Benefit 1: Work in a Distraction-Free Environment

A huge benefit of getting up early is that there are fewer distractions since most people are still asleep. You're unlikely to get phone calls early in the morning, and most work environments are free from background noise. Usually it's you, your thoughts and a singular focus on the important tasks.

Benefit 2: Plan Your Schedule for the Day

Rising early makes it possible for you to review scheduled appointments and plan other tasks before getting sucked into everyone else's agenda for the day.

Benefit 3: Complete the Most Important Tasks

The biggest advantage of getting up early is being able to focus on important tasks that require concentration. Often these activities are best done while you're still fresh. In many cases, they can be completed before most people even wake up. The benefit here is that, regardless of whatever happens during the day, you've tackled the #1 priority on your schedule.

Benefit 4: Set the Tone for the Day

Getting up early sets the tone for the day. Instead of starting the day off stressed and rushed, your day can start in a calm manner. You knock out the important things and attack the rest of the day with a clear mind and sense of purpose.

IMPLEMENTATION

If you're a night owl, you may balk at the idea of rising early, thinking that this is just for "morning people." However, you can train yourself to get up at a moderately early time.

For instance, Steve has never been a morning person. In the past, he would stay up until 3:00 in the morning and usually crawl out of bed at 10 a.m. It wasn't until he adopted the writing habit that he realized the importance of starting the day on the right foot. Now he gets up on most days between 6:30 to 7:30 am and starts his day with a solid block of writing.

He was able to do this by creating a morning routine that includes the following:

#1: Expose yourself to bright light by opening the shades if the sun is already up; using a "happy light," which is a full-spectrum light, for five minutes while doing something else such as eating breakfast; or using a full-spectrum light alarm clock that simulates the sun rising in your bedroom.

#2: Clean up by washing your face, brushing your teeth or taking a quick shower. This act signals to your brain that a new day has begun.

#3: Hydrate yourself by drinking at least eight ounces of water (with or without slices of citrus fruit) or herbal tea. If you're a coffee drinker, go ahead and have a cup of coffee as well, but don't skimp on water since it's necessary for hydration.

#4: Have something to eat. A big breakfast isn't necessary, and in fact can slow you down and make you feel sluggish. Instead of having a big breakfast, try something small such as a piece of fruit, a breakfast bar, yogurt with granola or nuts, an egg on a high-fiber muffin, or a healthy smoothie.

#5: Get your blood moving by doing a quick burst of exercise such as walking up and down your stairs 10 times, stretching your major muscle groups, performing three yoga pose sequences, doing 25 jumping jacks or creating your own mini exercise routine.

Steve typically walks for 10 to 15 minutes before starting the rest of his day.

#6: Connect with your passion. This is the final energizing activity that can serve as a bridge toward taking action on your tasks for the day. Some suggestions for this include reading a blog post about an area of interest, praying or meditating about your goals or reading a journal that tracks your progress toward a breakthrough goal. The goal for this step is to put you in the mood to take action.

This energizing morning ritual works best when it's completed in less than 30 minutes. The main purpose of this time is to wake you up and put you in the proper frame of mind to tackle the rest of your day.

What NOT to Do in the Morning

Now that you're awake, it's important to spend your time wisely, in a purposeful manner, and avoid doing things that zap your energy.

No matter how tempted you are, avoid surfing the Internet, watching television, going on social media sites or listening to the radio during the first part of the day. Save those things for midday breaks, or put them off until evening.

It's important to nicely explain to anyone who lives with you the importance of this time and why you need to be left alone until you've completed your morning tasks.

Build up Slowly

Finally, you'll set yourself up for failure if you try to get up three hours earlier than normal. Instead, start off by getting up 10 to 15 minutes early. Once that becomes a routine, make it another 10 to 15 minutes. Do this until you find that sweet spot where you wake up early without too much fatigue.

Challenge #2: Not Getting Things Done

It has often been said that time is our most valuable commodity. This is true in the sense that you can generate more of everything else in life, but there's no way to generate more time.

Regardless of whether you're rich or poor, regardless of your education level and regardless of where you live in the world, you have the same 1,440 minutes in a day that everyone else has.

The key, therefore, is to not focus on making more time, but to manage the time that you do have. This is especially true for entrepreneurs because the work we need to complete never ends. If you don't knowhow to unplug and recharge, then you'll burn out.

In this section, we talk about the second major challenge entrepreneurs face: managing time and maximizing productivity. You can overcome this obstacle by developing the following habits:

- ESH #6: Block time
- ESH #7: Batch tasks
- ESH #8: Take frequent breaks
- ESH #9: Maintain multiple lists
- ESH #10: Set actionable goals
- ESH #11: Find your productive "sweet spot"
- ESH #12: Track your progress

- ESH #13: Reduce mindless consumption
- ESH #14: Create disconnect time
- ESH #15: Focus on your strengths
- ESH #16: Set yourself apart

As entrepreneurs, we're often pulled in a million different directions. That's why you need to be strategic with time, focusing on what gets results for your business. In this section, we cover 11 Entrepreneur Success Habits that will help you do this.

ESH #6: Block Time

Multitasking, once thought to be a positive trait, has now been proven to decrease productivity. While multitasking, your brain shifts from one topic to another, which takes time. Sometimes that brain shift takes a microsecond, and other times it may take a few minutes to get back to where you were before you were interrupted. No matter what, there is *always* some loss of time.

The reality of multitasking is that you're giving only half (or less) of your attention to each task. This negatively impacts your ability to do anything well. In fact, according to a Stanford study (http://news.stanford.edu/news/2009/august24/multitask-research-study-082409.html), people who multitask underperform in EVERY area. For instance, multitasking results in, among other things, impaired memory.

Rebecca used to pride herself on her ability to multitask and wore multitasking as a badge of honor. She always kept several email tabs open at the top of her Web browser so she would immediately know when a new email came in from one of her clients.

Eventually she realized there was something wrong with this approach. In spite of starting work at 6:00 a.m. and often working until 11:00 p.m., Rebecca seldom made much progress on her to-do list, no matter how hard she worked. Her constant interruptions via email meant she frantically ran from one request to the next, which left her unfocused on the most important tasks.

On top of that, her constant interruptions meant that she often stopped in the middle of a sentence when writing an email to respond to an urgent need that came in via a different email. This resulted in confusion about what she had actually finished and what still needed her attention. It wasn't uncommon to find half-written emails in her drafts folder, days after she thought she had sent them.

The bottom line is that if you're regularly multitasking, regardless of how hard you work, you're likely putting out inferior work.

One of the best ways to break free from multitasking madness and avoid distractions is to block out your workday into small blocks of time and then work uninterrupted, completely focused on one specific task during that block of time.

During this time, you *don't* check email, hop on Facebook, send text messages or switch between projects. You simply focus on the <u>one task</u> you've chosen for that specific block of time.

Time blocking enables you to take control of your time and get the most important tasks done.

IMPLEMENTATION

There are three actions you can take to overcome the multitasking habit:

Action 1: Block out your ideal week. Your ideal week should include a mix of business and personal time. Rather than putting huge blocks of time such as "work" on your calendar, be more specific and block out time for certain major task categories on your calendar.

For instance, Steve blocks out time for writing, social media, working on projects, personal commitments and even his marathon training runs. Even though he works for himself, he finds that this regimented schedule helps him stay focused on the current activity.

When starting out, you don't necessarily have to block out a whole week. Try doing it at the beginning of each day. Then, once you're comfortable with this habit, spend a few hours one day to plan out the forthcoming week.

Action 2: Try the Pomodoro Technique. Both Steve and Rebecca use the Pomodoro Technique (http://pomodorotechnique.com/) to help them focus during their blocks of time. This technique was created by a man named Francesco Cirillo in the mid-1980s. He discovered that focusing intently on a specific task for a short period of time and then taking a short break increased focus and resulted in getting more done.

Here's how it works:

1. Create a list of tasks you want to complete for the day or during a specific block of time.
2. Put those tasks in priority order.
3. Set a timer for 25 minutes.
4. Work on the first task on your list until the timer goes off.
5. Make note of the first Pomodoro as a completed task.
6. Take a five-minute break. During this break, get up and move around. You can grab a cup of coffee, do some stretching exercises, or take care of a quick household chore such as emptying the dishwasher. The main thing is to have a complete mental break from the task you were working on, and to walk away from the computer.
   To keep your five-minute break from turning into a fifteen-minute or longer break, be sure to set a timer for five minutes.
7. Start the second Pomodoro, picking up where you left off on your task list.
8. Repeat this process. Once you've completed four Pomodoros, take a 15- to 30- minute break.
9. Continue this process until you've accomplished the most important tasks for your day.

If you follow the Pomodoro Technique strictly, one of the "rules" is that there is no such thing as a half a Pomodoro. If you're interrupted, you have to start the Pomodoro over again. While this may seem extreme, the reason for this rule is that it trains you to block out distractions and interruptions, and focus intently on the task at hand.

If you work around other people, you'll need to explain the Pomodoro Technique to them so they'll understand why you need to work uninterrupted.

For instance, Rebecca's husband works at home with her, and it's natural for them to converse throughout the day. Since she's explained the Pomodoro Technique to him, he knows exactly what she's talking about when she says, "I'm in the middle of a Pomodoro," and gives her the space she needs to complete it, knowing that she'll check in with himduring her break.

It takes time to adjust to the Pomodoro Technique, but you'll find that, once you get used to it, it will really help you get into the zone and get more done.

Action 3: Use the "One Tab" method. Having only one tab open on your computer at a time is a great way to reduce the temptation to multitask.

As an example, if you've blocked out time for email, then leave this tab open and close everything else. If you're updating a financial spreadsheet, have nothing but the spreadsheet open and close all other tabs. Simple, right?

Obviously, if you need other tabs to complete a current task, then leave them open. If you're updating a financial spreadsheet, you may need to have the spreadsheet and your online bank statement open, but you wouldn't need to open tabs for Facebook or email.

ESH #7: Batch Tasks

Batching tasks goes hand in hand with the previous discussion of time blocking. In a sense, it takes that habit and *turns it up to 11*.

With this habit, you lump similar tasks together and do them in batches, or in bulk, so that you can work in the most efficient manner.

For example, it makes more sense to make a batch of cookies than it does to bake a single cookie at a time. This is true because, regardless of how many cookies you make, you have to go through the same process of pulling out the ingredients, measuring, mixing things together, baking and cleaning up.

There are many positive outcomes associated with batching small items that could easily fall through the cracks if not batched with other tasks. Grouping smaller tasks together also makes it easier to get into the habit of doing them, since doing one small task can trigger the next task in the batch.

You'll be less likely to procrastinate since you don't have to think of what to do next—you simply do the next small task on the list.

Also, knocking these small items out in a single batch can free up more time, not to mention mental focus that can be devoted to accomplishing bigger tasks.

Here are some ways you can apply the same principle to your business:

Idea 1: If you're using the Pomodoro Technique, you can batch several small tasks together and complete them in one Pomodoro. Each task might only take a few minutes to complete. For best results, batch similar items such as responding to blog comments and responding to social media messages.

Idea 2: Batch tasks requiring a lot of mental strength together so you can give them your complete focus instead of shifting gears between different types of tasks.

For example, Rebecca writes three blog posts per week for one of her clients. She finds it easiest to work on those posts only one day per week. Doing so enables her to get into the groove of writing a specific type of content.

Idea 3: Steve and Rebecca both schedule all of their phone appointments, coaching calls, mastermind meetings and interviews for Wednesdays. This works well because that leaves the rest of the week free to focus on tasks that take a lot of focus, such as writing.

IMPLEMENTATION

You can apply this habit in a few different ways:

Action 1: Batch daily and weekly tasks. Certain tasks (like checking email) can be batched on a daily basis. Depending on how much time a task takes, you may want to block out one or two Pomodoros to complete it.

Weekly tasks may include making phone calls, running errands, making sales presentations in a certain region or updating your bookkeeping.

The more you block out your time into similar tasks, the more flexibility you'll have with the rest of your workweek.

Action 2: Schedule an office day. Once a week (or every other week), set aside time to take care of random odds and ends. Use this time to complete miscellaneous tasks that come up during the week.

Keep an ongoing list for your office day. Doing so makes it easier to remember important tasks without worrying about them while you are working on other things. When office day rolls around, prioritize the tasks and complete them in order.

Action 3: Perform small tasks in a logical sequence. Create a list of small items that are related or that make sense to do in a sequence.

For example, Steve follows what he calls a "habit stacking routine" where he batches together a series of important tasks to start the day. This includes drinking a vitamin-rich smoothie, focusing on energy-renewal activities, reviewing his goals and checking important business metrics. By the time he sits down to write, he's already completed a number of important habits.

Once you've made your list of small tasks that are similar in action and outcome, group them together in a logical order and create a process for doing them.

Try to create a sequence that takes approximately 25 minutes to complete, and then schedule a block of time to complete the tasks in a single Pomodoro.

While it may seem obsessive to add basic things such as taking vitamins to a checklist, Steve's found that batching those small things together makes them easier to remember. It also gives him a psychological boost, as checking those items off a list gives him a series of small wins so that, when he sits down to write, he feels energized and motivated to start working.

ESH #8: Take Frequent Breaks

If you're an entrepreneur who makes a living primarily sitting at a desk, you could potentially be sitting yourself to death. That may sound extreme, but there is actual evidence to back up that statement.

According to the JAMA Network (http://archinte.jamanetwork.com/article.aspx?articleid=1108810), six percent of global deaths are caused by inactivity. This appears to be true regardless of other health factors such as gender, age and body mass index.

This study shows the importance of exercising throughout the day. It doesn't matter if you spend an hour or two at the gym; it's still not healthy to sit for hours on end. There are many reasons why this is true, but one of the most significant is the way prolonged sitting impacts metabolic function. It also increases triglycerides levels, increases cholesterol and decreases insulin sensitivity.

Even if you exercise at other times of the day, it's still important to get up and move around throughout the workday.

If you happen to make a living sitting at a desk, like both Steve and Rebecca do, the solution is to get up and move around throughout the day. Not only do these breaks help to recharge your physical and mental batteries, they can also make a true difference in your overall health and well-being.

You may think you're getting a lot done as a result of staying focused and working away hour after hour, but if you keep grinding away, it's easy to lose concentration and not stayed 100 percent focused on what you need to accomplish. As a result, failing to take frequent breaks may even decrease your productivity.

IMPLEMENTATION

You can take frequent breaks throughout your workday without it negatively impacting your productivity. Here are few ways to make this happen:

Action 1: Move around between Pomodoros. By now you've probably realized we're both fans of the Pomodoro technique. In addition to helping you get more work done in less time, another fantastic aspect of this technique is that it encourages movement throughout the day.

By default, you have five minutes between each Pomodoro and a thirty-minute break after completing four of these blocks. This gives you plenty of time to move around. With the five-minute breaks, we encourage you to get out of the chair and do a quick walk around your work environment. Then, when it comes time for the 30-minute break, go outside and get some fresh air. You can even grab a pair of headphones and listen to a podcast as you get exercise.

An alternative to using the Pomodoro Technique is to set frequent timers that go off throughout the day. These will act as a reminder to get up and move around. A great app for this is Mind Jogger (https://itunes.apple.com/us/app/mind-jogger/id409841508?mt=8), which you can use to create random reminders at pre-scheduled intervals during the day.

Finally, it's also important to reward yourself in such a way that requires you to get up and move around.

After completing a certain amount of work, such as a single Pomodoro, you might reward yourself by getting up and brewing a cup of your favorite tea.

Action 2: Move around or complete quick exercise sets throughout the day. Walk up and down the stairs, stretch your muscles or do any other type of exercise you prefer. One thing Rebecca likes to do is to take a break and take her dog for a walk. The type of activity you do really doesn't matter. The important thing is to be intentional about taking frequent breaks.

You'd be surprised at the cumulative impact of completing small blocks of exercise throughout the day. Add them up and you'll see that they total more than 30 minutes of daily movement.

ESH #9: Maintain Multiple Lists

A Chinese proverb states that the weakest ink is better than the strongest memory. This is certainly true because, unless you write things down, you're likely to forget many of the great ideas that pop into your head.

Furthermore, attempting to store everything in your head can be very stressful. In fact, we all experience the overwhelm that happens when you have a lot of things on your mind. You know you have to do a dozen other things, so your mind is not fully focused on the task at hand.

If you're feeling that overwhelm, or too many things are slipping through the cracks, then your best bet is to create and maintain multiple lists for the different areas of your life. Below are six steps for getting started with managing your time with lists.

Step 1: Create projects for every area of your life.

Most likely you have projects you need to complete in several different aspects of your life. For instance, you may want to run a marathon, update your financial records, remodel your kitchen and write that "great American novel." Each of these should be treated as a project, with an individual task list for each project.

You should maintain these project lists in a central location—in a three-ring binder, in a program like Evernote or as individual folders in a filing cabinet.

Step 2: Break large tasks into bite-sized tasks.

People procrastinate for many reasons. Sometimes it's caused by laziness, but many times procrastination is a result of not clearly defining a set of steps. This often happens when a project is so big that you simply don't know where to start.

To get past this, the best course of action is to jot down every single task that needs to be done for every project.

These individual tasks should be small enough that they can be done in a single sitting so that, when you look at your project list, it's not overwhelming to think of everything you have to complete.

John Turner, CEO of UsersThink (http://usersthink.com/), sets goals for each day and then creates a task list based on those goals.

He says, "This precise focus on that day, and only making goals for the next day after that day is over, gives me an advantage over others, as it gives me flexibility to adjust around unforeseen obstacles and opportunities. This helps me move much faster than others who only look at the 'big' goals."

The key here is that he creates lists based on bigger goals, which helps him focus on the important things.

Step 3: Show only certain tasks.

To combat overwhelm, you can take a project list full of actions and use filters to show only the tasks you need to complete on a specific day.

For instance, before starting a workday (or even better, the night before), mark a few key tasks as high priority and then filter your list to only show the tasks that have been marked as high priority. That way, you focus on only the most important items without being distracted and getting overwhelmed by seeing the larger task list.

If you've set up your project lists (and associated tasks) in a three-ring binder, review the tasks you need to complete and add the ones for your next workday to another list. Then close the binder and put it away until you start planning for the next day.

Step 4: Set specific deadlines.

Deadlines create a sense of urgency. Even if there isn't an actual deadline for a task, give it a due date so you'll have a sense of urgency for completing the task.

Step 5: Evaluate your project list.

As entrepreneurs, we all have random moments of inspiration. Some of these ideas often turn into projects. The problem? When you keep adding projects to your list without closing previous ones, you'll end up with a very long list of things to do.

You'll also find that some projects keep getting pushed to the bottom of the list. To keep your project list fresh, skim through it on occasion.

When you notice that certain projects have been on the list a very long time, evaluate whether or not you want to keep focusing on them. Just because you wanted to do something at one time doesn't mean it's the best thing for you to do now. Don't be afraid to eliminate ideas that are no longer relevant.

On the other hand, if fear, laziness or insecurity is keeping you from tackling a project, it may be good to move it to the top of your list so you can knock it out sooner rather than later.

Step 6: Create checklists for routine activities.

It may seem silly to create a checklist for tasks you do on a routine basis, but having a checklist forces you to take action, especially if the specific tasks are easy to complete. Also, a checklist keeps you from forgetting to do an important step that may fall through the cracks if you don't write it down.

For instance, Rebecca uses a checklist for her blog posts. Most of the items would be done regardless of whether or not they are on a list, but having a pre-established process makes it easy to remember every mini action. It also gives her a sense of accomplishment to put a checkmark next to another item that has been completed for the day.

IMPLEMENTATION

We've just gone over a six-step process for maintaining multiple lists, but here is a simple plan for building the list-making habit.

Action 1: Set up a system for your projects. This will be a place to keep track of all of the projects you are working on. You can use a project management system such as Asana (https://asana.com/) or Basecamp (https://basecamp.com/), a task list such as the ones in Gmail or Outlook, or a three-ring binder.

The main thing is to have a place to keep track of all of the projects and tasks you need to complete.

Action 2: Jot down a list of potential projects for different areas of your life. This list should include items from your business *and* your personal life.

Action 3: Take each of the projects you jotted down in the previous step and break them down into small, individual tasks. Create checklists for the tasks that you do on a regular basis, and add those to your project management system (e.g., Basecamp or your three-ring binder).

Action 4: At the end of your workday (or first thing in the morning), plan out the most important tasks that need to be completed. Then start the day by focusing on these activities.

ESH #10: Set Actionable Goals

Are you a goal setter? If not, you should be. The most successful entrepreneurs in the world regularly set (and achieve) dynamic goals.

While it's great to work with a daily task list, a task list is not enough. In fact, if you create a task list every day that isn't based on goals, then you'll waste time working very hard without getting anywhere.

As entrepreneurs, we believe it's important to have goals in every area of your life, not just your business. Otherwise, it's easy to grow your business while having other areas of your life fall into shambles. Life is seldom perfect. However, when you're intentional about setting goals in multiple areas, you move a little closer toward a good work-life balance.

Getting back to the original point—goal setting gives you a sense of purpose for the tasks you do on a daily basis. The key is to make sure that each action relates to a long-term plan. You'll be motivated when you know that a specific task moves you one step closer to achieving an important goal.

If you've created goals in the past (and had very little success), then you should focus on setting S.M.A.R.T. goals.

S.M.A.R.T. is an acronym for: **S**pecific, **M**easurable, **A**ttainable, **R**elevant and **T**ime-bound.

Here's how it works:

S: Specific.

One of the most important aspects of S.M.A.R.T goals is that they are specific. If a goal is not specific, it is impossible to know if what you're doing is helping you accomplish the goal.

One of the best ways to create specific goals is to ask the six W questions: who, what, where, when, which and why.

When you answer these questions, it's very easy to create goals that have a measurable outcome.

- Who is involved?

- What do I want to accomplish?
- Where will I complete the goal?
- When do I want to do it?
- Which requirements and constraints might get in my way?
- Why am I doing it?

Here's a great example of a specific goal:

"This month, I will create a 30-page document that outlines a plan for creating three new streams of income for my business. These new income streams will increase my income by 25 percent."

There is no ambiguity in the above goal. The outcome is very clear. By the end of the month, you've either completed this 30-page document or you haven't.

M: Measurable

Another important ingredient is to make each goal measurable.

For example, the above goal includes figures that can be measured. Instead of just stating that you will write a document, you give a specific number—30 pages long. Also, instead of stating a vague desire for additional income streams, the goal specifically describes how three additional income streams will be added and how much revenue they will generate.

A: Attainable

One big mistake people make is setting goals that have little to no chance of success.

Let's talk about the previous example. A 30-page document can be realistically completed in 30 days. Generating a 25 percent increase in income is also an attainable goal.

However, if your business generated $50,000 in revenue last year, then it would be a mistake to create a $1 million goal for the upcoming year.

This isn't to say you shouldn't create challenging goals. Just make sure that, with a good degree of effort, you can actually accomplish each goal on your list.

Finally, each future goal should be progressively more challenging. For example, you may want your next goal to be based on a 30 percent increase in income. Then rinse and repeat with another percentage increase goal. Keep doing this until you hit financial numbers that put you among the top entrepreneurs in your industry.

R: Relevant

Your goals must be relevant to what you want to accomplish. They should fit with your desires and passions. Don't create goals that are focused on trying to please your parents, your spouse, your children or other people in your life.

If the goals you create are not based on what you truly want to do, it will be difficult to stick with them.

T: Time-bound

Each goal should have a specific timeframe for completion. You can set a specific due date or just specify that you will achieve a goal within a particular month or financial quarter.

Steve likes to set two goals, with one of the goals being a short-term goal for the next month and one a long-term goal to complete within the next three months. He prefers the immediacy of these goals because it's easier to stay focused and not get distracted by other projects.

Goals for the Whole Person

As mentioned earlier, your goals shouldn't focus solely on business. They should also cover the rest of your life. This is important because you'll run every new opportunity through a filter of how it will impact your other obligations. This will help you make better decisions about what you're *actually* able to accomplish.

You should set goals for the following:

- Education (both formal and informal)
- Career or business
- Hobbies and recreation
- Health and fitness
- Relationships
- Spirituality
- Finances
- Public service

Another mistake many people make is trying to do too much all at once. For example, some people try to set goals for all eight areas described above. Unfortunately, it's very difficult to reach eight major goals in the same timeframe. Instead of trying to tackle everything at once, set goals that cover two or three areas of your life. After a few months, review your goal list. If you feel something is lacking in another area of your life, create another goal to address the problem.

Finally, it's important to understand the **two *types* of goals** and the impact they have on your ability to get things done.

First there are performance goals. With this type of goal, you focus on the effort instead of a specific outcome. A performance goal would be something like, "During the month of June, I will go to the gym 12 times."

Next are outcome goals that shoot for a specific metric. For example, an outcome goal would be something like "By the end of June, I will be able to bench press 200 pounds."

In most cases, it is best to focus on performance goals rather than outcome goals. The important thing is to develop the habit of taking action on a daily basis. Outcome goals can lead to discouragement if you fail to meet the goals. Performance goals are much better because they keep you focused on the process and are more within your control to achieve.

For instance, even if you go to the gym 12 times during the month of June, you still may not be able to bench press 200 pounds by the end of the month. This can be very discouraging when you've given it your best effort. If you focus on performance goals, it's much more likely that you'll be able to accomplish your goals and stay motivated to continue.

IMPLEMENTATION

Here is a simple action plan for turning S.M.A.R.T. goals into a regular habit:

1. Think of what you'd like to achieve in the next three months.
2. Write down S.M.A.R.T. goals for two to three of areas of your life.
3. Create an action plan for each goal.
4. Review these goals on a daily basis.
5. When reviewing current projects, focus on ones that directly relate to a goal.
6. If a project doesn't relate to one of your goals, eliminate it.
7. At the end of the three months, evaluate your overall success.
8. Create new goals and make them more challenging.

ESH #11: Maximize Your Productive "Sweet Spot"

Are you naturally a morning person? Or are you a night owl who comes alive at midnight and works well into the evening?

While there are many benefits to rising early (as mentioned in ESH #5), the real key is to find when you are the most productive and use that time to the fullest.

For instance, Rebecca is naturally a morning person and tends to get up early and get right to work. She finds that if she doesn't get started on things early in the morning, she most likely won't get much done. Her husband is just the opposite and tends to work best in the evening, sometimes staying up most of the night to work on projects.

Neither way is right or wrong. The important thing is to be intentional in the work you do, and to do your most important tasks during your most productive time of day whenever possible. Here are five steps for getting started:

Step 1: Identify your ideal work environment.

Some people work well in a noisy coffee shop with a lot of noise around. Others prefer a quiet, or perhaps even silent, atmosphere.

While you may not be able to control your work environment 100 percent of the time, it's important to figure out what works best for you. Maximize your productivity by spending as much time as possible in your ideal work environment during your most productive time of day.

Step 2: Embrace the "80/20 Rule."

As mentioned above, you need to focus on the most important tasks during your peak times. Before we go further, it's important to define what is meant by "most important" tasks.

One of the best ways to do this is to follow the 80/20 principle. This is a principle that was initially observed by Vilfredo Pareto (and thus is also commonly referred to as the Pareto Principle). Pareto said you get 80 percent of your results from 20 percent of your efforts. This means that the bulk of your success comes from only a handful of the tasks you do.

To have the best results, you need to first identify your 80/20 tasks. When it comes to running a business, these tasks are the ones that impact your bottom line—your paycheck. They are the items that generate income for your business.

This is going to be different for everyone, so don't let others define your 80/20 tasks for you. Other people often have an agenda that may not match up with yours. If you let them dictate your focus, you might end up derailing your productivity.

Step 3: Delegate, eliminate and learn to say "no."

As an entrepreneur, you may be tempted to do everything on your own. After all, for most of us, there are limits to how much we can afford to spend on hiring help. But hiring help, especially in the areas where you aren't the most gifted, can free you up to focus on "sweet spot" activities—the tasks that energize you and that no one else can do quite like you.

There may be some tasks you can't delegate (either because you don't have the budget or can't find a qualified person). If that's the case, then it's important to determine whether or not that task really needs to be done. If not, then eliminate it.

It's also important to learn to say no when a request is made or an "opportunity" is presented to you that doesn't fit with what you know is best for you. Saying no can be difficult, especially if you're a people pleaser, but it's essential if you want to stay in your sweet spot.

Step 4: Focus on one thing.

The 80/20 principle is a great place to start, but it can be helpful to dig even deeper. When it comes to running a successful business, you need to determine the "one thing" that is your most important activity. This activity should be the primary focus of your workday.

The book *The One Thing* (http://www.developgoodhabits.com/the-one-thing) by Gary Keller and Jay Papasan is a great example of the power of a single activity. It's based on the premise that your best results come from a consistent effort on a single activity.

For Steve, that one thing is writing more books. He doesn't consider himself a natural writer, but over the last two years he has determined that writing is the most important thing he needs to do on a daily basis.

As a result, Steve writes an average of 2,000 words per day. Because of his focus on writing, he has published more than 40 Kindle books and built an entire business around the Kindle platform. His success with Kindle wouldn't have happened if, instead of making a point of writing each day, he started the day by answering emails or focusing on activities that other people deem to be most important.

Step 5: Take back your work time.

If you're still working a day job, your boss might define your priority tasks for you. In that situation, you need to do what others (e.g., supervisors) have deemed most important.

However, you may be able to approach your boss with a detailed plan regarding your most important tasks. If you explain how spending time on these tasks can actually increase your productivity and improve the company's bottom line, you may be given a little more freedom to set your own priorities.

For instance, when Rebecca was still working a day job, she found it difficult to get things done because of frequent interruptions that occurred throughout the day. She knew she could get more done if she had some alone time, but at the same time, people depended on her being at her desk.

She proposed the following solution to both her immediate supervisor and her company's HR director:

There were some offices in the building where she worked that were not being used. They were located in an out-of-the-way place, on a wing where people didn't go too often. Rebecca's proposal was that she be allowed to work on her most important tasks one day per week in a "secret" office that only her boss, the few coworkers in her department and the HR director knew about. She knew that having limited (but concentrated) amounts of alone time to focus on the most important things would make her more productive, which would benefit the company.

Since those who needed her most (e.g., her boss and direct coworkers) knew where she was and how to reach her, and since this work arrangement still kept her at her own desk a great deal of the time, her proposal was a success.

IMPLEMENTATION

Here is a simple action plan for maximizing your productive "sweet spot."

Action 1: Identify your periods of peak productivity. Spend a week writing down the times of day when you feel most energized and productive. If you're unsure, think back to the days when you got the most done and note when that work was accomplished.

Action 2: Identify your "one thing." Examine your business closely to determine the #1 activity that produces the biggest results. It could be making sales calls, consulting with clients, writing or creating high-leverage content. Whatever drives your business forward is your one thing.

Action 3: Create a schedule around that one thing.

First, focus on completing the most important thing during your ideal work time, when you're at a peak level of energy. For some, this will be first thing in the morning. For others, it will be late at night when everyone else is asleep. The key here is to spend your peak time on the one activity that's critical for the success of your business.

Next, use the rest of your workday to complete other tasks that produce the best results for your business. Work on the 80 percent (less important) tasks later in the day. If you don't have enough time at the end of the day, then you know you've only missed out on activities that aren't critical to your success.

Action 4: Start the day with an important question. Ask yourself, "What's the one thing I need to do today to consider this day to be a success?"

Most likely, it will be the activity you've chosen as the "one thing." But on occasion, there may be a different task that is more urgent. Regardless of what it is, be intentional about getting that one thing done so you can end the day with a feeling of accomplishment.

ESH #12: Track Your Progress

It's essential to measure the important metrics for your business; otherwise, you have no real way of knowing if the actions you take are generating any results.

For example, Rebecca once tried blogging every day, seven days per week. After hearing about some other bloggers who tried this with great results, she wanted to see if doing so would increase her Web traffic and boost her bottom line.

She found that blogging daily increased traffic, but it wasn't commensurate with the amount of time and effort it took to do so. Instead of increasing her income, it decreased it, since it reduced the amount of time she had to devote to other income-producing activities.

She wouldn't have known this if she didn't pay attention to key metrics such as her website traffic versus total monthly income.

Revisiting the 80/20 Principle

In the previous chapter, we explored the importance of the 80/20 principle. The bottom line is that there is no way to even know which actions are most important if you don't focus on milestones and track measurable results.

In the above example, Rebecca discovered that she was putting 80 percent of her effort into writing blog posts, but she didn't see a lot of progress toward completing her most important goals. She decided to shift her blog writing—which she still deems as important—to a lower time commitment. She now uses 80 percent of her writing time producing income-generating assets and the other 20 percent producing posts for her blog.

Track the Most Important Metrics

It's easy for entrepreneurs to get caught up in things that don't matter. For instance, a blogger may become hyper-focused on blog comments or social media shares, even though you can't take comments or the number of times your blog post has been shared on Twitter to the bank!

On the other hand, tracking the number of people who opt-in to an email list and then tracking how many people make a purchase as a result of the emails you send does make a difference when it comes to your business' bottom line.

It also makes more sense to track the amount of work you get done in a specific period instead of the number of hours you work. For one business owner, that may mean tracking the number of sales made in a day versus the number of hours worked. For another business owner, it might make sense to track the number of words written in a day rather than the number of hours spent sitting in front of the computer.

Naturally, one vital metric is the amount of income you bring in each month as a result of all the work you do.

Set Deadlines

When starting a project that will require a big chunk of time, it's important to set a deadline for evaluating its overall success. For example, Rebecca focused on daily blogging for 30 days before deciding that doing so wasn't worth it.

It's important for the deadline to be long enough to provide enough data to evaluate, but short enough that you don't waste too much time on something that isn't working.

Celebrate Milestones

One of the best things you can do to stay motivated in the areas that are most important in your business is to celebrate milestones.

For example, have you ever been in a store or restaurant and seen a dollar bill in a frame? That dollar bill, while a small amount of money, was very significant because it was the first dollar earned by the company. Earning that first dollar was a milestone in the company's history.

Here are some examples of milestones to celebrate:

- The first dollar you make from a specific source (e.g., advertising income, the sale of a new product or service, etc.).
- Certification or some other type of accomplishment that will differentiate you from your competition.
- A specific number of monthly website visitors.
- Learning a new skill that will produce a new income opportunity.
- Getting hired by a top client.
- Being asked to guest post on a top blog.
- Landing a speaking engagement at a conference in your industry.

Set Realistic Milestones

If your milestones are too lofty, you end up feeling like a failure—even if you make great progress. It's great to dream big, but don't forget to break your aspirations down into small milestones. That way you can see obvious evidence of your progress without feeling like a failure.

IMPLEMENTATION

There is a simple two-step action plan for developing the habit of tracking your progress:

Step 1: Quantify the important metrics.

Every business is driven by important metrics (like revenue, expenditures and customer acquisition costs). Unfortunately, it's easy to fall into the trap of worrying about "vanity metrics" that might look good but don't actually help your business (like the number of comments on your latest blog post). Only consider the things that actually drive your business forward and learn to proactively ignore the rest.

For instance, Steve's entire business is driven by three core metrics:

1. Total book sales per day
2. Total email subscribers
3. Conversion rates per source of traffic

While other metrics have some importance, Steve uses the 80/20 rule to focus on the activities that increases book sales and add subscribers to his email list. Every other task is secondary to these outcomes.

Step 2: Review your metrics on a regular basis.

Every week, carve out a few hours when you can go over everything and make sure the work you're doing is in line with your expectations. If you're a data junkie like Steve, you should track key metrics in an Excel spreadsheet that's maintained throughout the life of your business.

Also, spend time at the end of each day reviewing what you've accomplished. If there were things you didn't get done, decide whether or not those items should be scheduled for the next day, pushed back or eliminated. This goes back to your "one thing." If your day-to-day actions are not directly related to your key metrics, then you're probably wasting time.

Finally, at the end of the day, plan out the next day's tasks with an emphasis on the things that will help you reach your most important milestones.

Repeat this process until you're instinctively starting each day with a focus on the most important tasks.

ESH #13: Reduce Mindless Consumption

One thing that sets successful entrepreneurs apart from "wantrapreneurs" is that successful entrepreneurs understand the value of focusing on the things that truly matter. This often means reducing distractions and eliminating habits that hold them back. For example, a successful entrepreneur is unlikely to spend several hours per day watching television.

Now it's true that we all need to escape sometimes, and watching television or reading a mindless novel are great ways to do so. We all need that bit of escapism from time to time. The problem is when you fill your life with too many pointless activities, giving you a limited amount of time to work on your business. That's why it's important to reduce distractions in the following ways:

#1. Set limits on your "mindless consumption."

You don't need to eliminate mindless activities completely, but you should reduce them to a level that helps you recharge without keeping you from getting more important things done.

One way to make the most of these diversions is to set specific limits, such as watching no more than one hour of television per day. You can also pre-record certain shows and only watch them when you're relaxing. This will eliminate the bad habit of watching television for the sake of having nothing better to do.

#2. View mindless activities as a reward for hard work.

Another great option is to use mindless activities as a reward for getting work done. For example, the only time Steve watches television is when he's completed a full day's work, exercised and spent time with his fiancée. Usually this amounts to only one hour per day.

#3. Make adjustments according to your current season.

There are some seasons in the life of your business when you may need to push harder and get more done. For example, if you're launching a new product or opening a new location, you may be too busy and not have as much time for leisure activities.

Each season always transitions into another season, so there is always an end in sight. If you look at things through the lens of seasons, you'll be motivated to push extra hard for a period of time, knowing it won't last forever.

If, after pushing really hard in one season, you want to relax a bit more in the next season, be sure to define when the more relaxed season will end so that you don't allow it to go on longer than it ideally should.

IMPLEMENTATION

Here's a quick plan for reducing mindless consumption in your life:

Step 1: For a couple of weeks, keep track of the time you spend doing different activities. For instance, how much time you spend working on your most important tasks and how much time you spend on unessential items such as watching television and goofing off on sites such as YouTube.

If you waste a lot of time with online activities, then use software like Rescue Time (https://www.rescuetime.com/) to give you honest feedback on how much time you waste on each site.

Step 2: If you find yourself wasting a disproportionate amount of time on something like watching television (e.g., three to four hours per night), make a decision to cut back. It sounds brutal, but the best strategy is to go show by show and really decide if watching is worth what it costs in lost business productivity.

Step 3: Consider blocking out time for work and time for play. If you spend very little time watching television, you may want to give yourself time to watch a show or two one day per week.

Step 4: Pick a handful of shows you want to watch or mindless novels you want to read. Then make time for them in your schedule. If you want to watch a few shows, use a service like TiVo or DVR to record shows during the week and watch them at your leisure. Don't watch them until you've completed more important tasks.

ESH #14: Create "Disconnect Time"

It was once believed that technology could help us all save time. In theory, that's true, but the reality is that many entrepreneurs are faced with very little time to disconnect and decompress.

Compare this to how it used to be (especially in a traditional job). When you left work for the day, you *really* left work and didn't have to think about it until you walked in the door the next morning.

In contrast, there is now is an expectation that you'll have your phone with you at all times and be able to respond to emails and texts at all hours of the day. That's why it's important to create "disconnect time" by doing two things:

#1. Train Your Clients.

Whether it's intentional or not, your behavior trains clients to expect certain things from you. The "training" can be either good or bad.

For example, Rebecca used to check her email all the time. Her clients made statements such as, "You always respond to me so quickly, I feel like I'm your only client."

This seems like a good thing, but it came with a heavy price tag because it created the expectation that Rebecca would always respond right away. She could never disconnect without someone wondering why it took "so long" for her to get back to them.

In one situation, she was training a new team member to do a specific task. She intentionally kept her email open to be able to answer any questions or provide any help that was needed. One day she took a quick break and, 23 minutes later, received multiple emails from the teammate (and a text from another teammate) stating that no one could find her.

While the expectations of her teammates were unrealistic, Rebecca herself was the one responsible for creating those expectations in the first place.

Through that experience, she learned to train her clients to expect her to not be available during certain times. She did this by communicating with them about her boundaries and letting them know when to expect a response.

#2. Unplug Regularly.

Unplugging on a regular basis will help you focus on other things that matter, such as time with family, and help you recharge your batteries.

Just like you block out time to do certain tasks, make a habit of blocking out time to unplug.

For example, when going out with family or friends, consider turning the ringer off on your phone and not taking it out to look at it until you return home.

It can also be helpful to shut all electronics down an hour before bed so that you can better transition from work to sleep mode.

As an example, Steve recently created a habit where he stopped looking at his phone during the evening. When he gets home from exercising at night, he walks into his office, puts his phone on the charger and doesn't look at it until the next morning. If he wants to read an eBook, he uses the Kindle Paperwhite without connecting to the Internet.

You don't need to go to extreme measures like this, but it's important to think carefully about technology. Does it improve your life? Or do you constantly check your phone like an addict looking for that next fix? Only *you* know the answer to these questions. If constant connectivity negatively impacts your life, then it might be time to get extreme and proactively unplug on a regular basis.

IMPLEMENTATION

We've already covered two core strategies for unplugging, but here's a simple plan for implementing these ideas:

Action 1: Block off two hours of every day in your schedule, during which everyone knows not to interrupt you, schedule appointments for you or expect email responses from you. This could be in the morning when you're focusing on "the one thing."

Action 2: Create "office hours" when you can be reached via phone or email. This helps people know you're there to help them, but it puts you in control of your schedule.

Action 3: Block out time away from the computer. For instance, you may want to make Sunday a computer-free day and, instead of being online, spend the day relaxing outdoors, being renewed spiritually or spending time focused on the relationships that matter most to you.

You can take this one step further by disconnecting from technology for an hour every day and getting back to basics with some old school methods like writing out a plan using pen and paper.

Action 4: Be intentional about email. Instead of constantly monitoring your inbox, devote specific times to email processing. At all other times, don't look at your inbox unless you're expecting a specific business-related message.

Both Steve and Rebecca typically carve out large blocks of time in the morning where they don't access email, social media or even the Internet. This is when they're most creative, so they reserve this time for important tasks.

There are a few different ways you can properly manage your email:

- Have a VA filter and organize your messages before you even take a look at your inbox.
- Turn off the mailbox feature on your phone.
- Batch email processing activities together at one specific time of day.
- Focus on your "one thing" before demands that come through email and distractions that come through social media suck you in. In fact, pick one offline activity—such

as taking a walk—and do it before logging on to the Internet.

Email is an important part of an entrepreneur's life. However, it needs to be managed in a way that doesn't take too much time away from the "big picture" tasks. You can still complete high-priority items while staying in touch with important colleagues and clients. The trick is to set boundaries on your time and stick to a schedule.

ESH #15: Focus on Your Strengths

Many entrepreneurs have a "can do" attitude, which is often a requirement if you want to succeed. Unfortunately, this attitude often leads to a dangerous mindset where you feel like you need to do everything yourself.

For example, if you create all of your own content, do all your own bookkeeping, handle customer service and tweak your website design (even if you're not good at all those things), you end up hindering the growth of your business.

You need to bootstrap when you first start your business, but once money starts coming in, it's important to focus on your strengths and hire people to do everything else.

Think of it this way: If you focus on your weaknesses, not only does a task take longer to complete, but it won't be done as well as it would be if you let an expert do it. In fact, the time you spend on it could have been better spent working on the tasks you do better than anyone else.

To illustrate this point, let's talk about Chris Ducker and his 3 Lists to Freedom (http://www.chrisducker.com/3-lists-to-freedom/) concept.

This is an exercise that both Steve and Rebecca completed when attending a Business Breakthrough event with Chris Ducker and Pat Flynn. (It was this exercise that led Steve to hire his virtual assistant, Glori, who is now a valuable part of his team.)

Here's how this process works:

- Grab a piece of paper and a pen.
- Draw two lines down the middle of the paper to create three columns.
- In column #1, jot down whatever you hate doing on a day-to-day basis.

- In column #2, jot down what you're struggling with. These are tasks that need to get done, but you're not good at doing them.
- In column #3, jot down the tasks you shouldn't be doing. You may like doing these things, but they aren't the best use of your time and could be done by someone else.

After doing the exercise, you will have a list of tasks that can be delegated or outsourced.

Depending on where you're at financially, you may not be ready to hire someone for every item on this list. However, you can start with little projects and go from there.

If money is a big concern, you may also want to look into outsourcing to countries such as the Philippines because the cost is lower than it would be if you hired someone based in the United States.

For example, Rebecca has two part-time team members who are in the U.S. She has also used oDesk to hire people from differen countries. These people completed random tasks for her at a very low cost. This keeps her overall cost of outsourcing low but provides her with a good deal of support.

Steve hired a full-time VA through Chris Ducker's agency, Virtual Staff Finder (http://www.virtualstafffinder.com/). Because she is located in the Philippines, the cost is lower than it would be if he hired someone located in the U.S. He also has a handful of contractors in the U.S. and Canada who do work for him on a regular basis. Because they are independent contractors who work on a non-retainer basis, the cost is very reasonable.

Both Steve and Rebecca have found that paying others to do what they're not good at (or simply shouldn't be doing) is a great way to increase your bottom line and strengthen your overall brand. For example, neither one is a graphic designer, so they pay someone to design compelling book covers.

Keep in mind that some of the tasks on your plate may ideally be done partly by you and partly by someone else. For instance, Rebecca provides transcription services to a handful of her clients. While she is a fast typist and could do the transcription herself, she pays transcribers to do the actual typing. Then she edits the transcripts to make sure they are the best they can possibly be.

Focus on the Strengths of Your Company

In addition to focusing on your own strengths, it's also important to focus on the strengths of your company rather than trying to be everything to everyone.

Josh Nickell, owner of Nickell Rental (http://www.nickellrental.com/), writes, "I continually focus on what our business can do best. Many companies can be great at a few things, but the most successful companies keep a razor focus on what makes them the best. In the rental industry, there are many types of equipment you can rent and many customer types on which you can focus.

"Most of our success and profit is driven by serving small to midsize contractors and DIY homeowners. Many rental companies get distracted by segments of their industry they can't effectively serve. If a rental company rents tents, trucks, event equipment, tools, industrial equipment and production equipment, sells merchandise and retails new equipment, they will always struggle to create raving fans and consistency.

"Once you know where to focus your investment, it makes it easy to say no to projects or opportunities that aren't within the scope of your business. Projects outside your niche are then easy to distinguish, allowing you to focus all your available resources on projects that are likely to have higher payoffs and strengthen your core business. If I look at all my plans and ideas through the lens of whether it serves small to midsize contractors and DIY homeowners, I know I can get the best return on my investment.

"Let your competition battle over other opportunities. Not only will they struggle to compete with you in your targeted markets, but they will also be dealing with the constant distraction of competition and investment in other segments."

This is a great example of how focusing not just on your own personal strengths, but on the strengths of your business as a whole, can have a huge impact on your success.

IMPLEMENTATION

Here's a simple action plan for focusing on your strengths:

Action 1: Identify what some call your "Core Genius," which is nothing more than the handful of skills you can do better than anyone else.

Action 2: Complete Chris Ducker's "3 Lists to Freedom" exercise, specifically identifying the tasks that should be handled by someone else.

Action 3: Take the list of things you should outsource from the previous exercise and put them in order of priority. Then hire people who can handle those tasks for you. You can interview people in person (if you have an offline business) or hire them via a freelancing website.

Get started by checking out agencies such as Chris Ducker's Virtual Staff Finder. If you prefer an agency based in the U.S., eaHELP (http://www.eahelp.com/) and HireMyMom (http://hiremymom.com/) are two good ones to consider for hiring a virtual assistant.

Action 4: For one-off projects, you should check out oDesk (https://www.odesk.com/) and Elance (https://www.elance.com/). Both of those sites are great for finding people who can handle anything related to a computer, such as Web design, phone or online customer support, bookkeeping, etc. Rebecca has hired people on oDesk to handle things such as PowerPoint presentation creation and Steve has hired people on these sites for pretty much every type of task.

Action 5: Develop the delegation habit by consistently asking yourself "who is the best person for this task?" Then create a process where that person takes full responsibility for task completion.

If you already have a team in place, you may want to have them take a test such as StrengthsFinder (http://www.strengthsfinder.com/home.aspx) to identify the core competencies of your business. Write a statement outlining what your company is best at and begin to evaluate each opportunity on the basis of whether or not it fits your core strengths.

ESH #16: Set Yourself Apart

Customers are one thing; raving fans are quite another. You can get a few customers by doing the bare minimum, but you need to be exceptional in order to stand out from the competition.

Let's look at a non-glamorous industry as an example—fast food.

In some fast-food restaurants, you place an order and, when it's ready, they yell out your number and you grab the food at the counter. At other places, you sit down after placing your order and the food is brought to your table.

Now this is a small difference. Customers may not even be consciously aware of the difference between the two restaurants, but on a subconscious level you feel better about the second place because you received a little bit of extra service.

Continuing on with this example, most sit-down restaurants have no problem with two diners sharing a meal. They'll happily bring you an extra plate. The ones that stand out, however, divide the food for you and bring it out on two separate plates. This saves you from the rather messy process of dividing food at the table.

Here is another example of how a business sets itself apart:

At one clothing store, you're left to fend for yourself, hoping to find clothing that fits and looks good. Perhaps you walk around the store holding on to several items of clothing. Eventually it becomes uncomfortable and inconvenient to handle all these items, so you rush through the shopping experience.

In another clothing store, sales associates are there to help you. They identify clothing they think will look good, even bringing different sizes or styles as you try things on. If the initial selections aren't quite right, they keep bringing you new things.

With the second business example, customers feel better cared for and are more likely to enjoy the experience. Often this means they'll tell others about it and go back time and time again—even if they have to pay a little more.

It Doesn't Take That Much to Stand Out

When it comes to setting yourself apart, the primary requirement is a little bit of extra time and hustle. For instance, in the fast-food example, it may take an additional 15 to 30 seconds for food to be brought to the customer rather than yelling a name and leaving the food at the counter.

In other cases, there may be an additional cost, such as offering a free cup of coffee or tea while a customer waits for service. This requires a small expenditure on your part, yet it can have a big impact on how customers feel about your business.

A Personal Example...

The minimum bar with Amazon publishing is pretty low. Some books are just a few dozen pages long, and many are rife with spelling and grammatical errors. Other books are literally rehashed ideas stolen from other authors.

One of the reasons Steve's book platform stands out isn't because he's a genius, or even because writing comes naturally to him, but because he goes the extra mile.

For example, he writes multiple drafts, focuses on providing good content, makes sure each book is as error-free as possible (by hiring two professional editors) and pays for professional cover design so his books don't have the "self-published look" that's common on the Kindle platform.

In spite of the extra work and cost that goes into these books, he keeps his prices at the same rate as when he started out.

It hasn't always been this way for Steve. When he published his first few books, he didn't pay for professional editing and people quickly let him know (by leaving negative reviews) that he needed to improve his process.

He can attribute much of his current success to the single philosophy of going the extra mile and doing what many other Kindle authors don't do.

Practice Continuous Improvement

The thought of making multiple improvements all at once can be downright overwhelming.

One way to beat overwhelm is to practice Kaizen, which is Japanese for "good change." The basic idea here is to focus on continual improvements in small increments.

In Steve's case, the first step was professional cover design for his book. Next, he hired one editor. After that, he transitioned into having each book edited twice. Now he focuses on providing more actionable content in each book, which results in a higher word count.

IMPLEMENTATION

The following is a simple action plan for setting yourself apart from the competition:

Action 1: Study your competition and see if you can come up with ideas for improving on their processes.

Action 2: Listen to feedback from your customers and create a plan for implementing feedback, especially when the same theme comes up multiple times. In Steve's case, people left negative reviews because of typos, so he hired editors and focused on improving the quality of the reading experience.

Put yourself in your customers' shoes and ask yourself what you would want if you were in their place. Find out what they do and don't like. Then make a plan for adding those extra touches to your services or products.

Action 3: At least once a month, come up with one small improvement you can make for the business. The key is to focus on small improvements rather than worrying about big ones. For instance, if you don't currently have a phone number on your website and the only way people can get ahold of you is by email, you may decide to add a phone number to your contact page.

Create an ongoing list of these improvements. Remember the 80/20 rule when looking at this list. Identify the actions that will have the biggest positive impact on your business and implement those before doing anything else.

Challenge #3: Increasing Competition

We've all heard that the Einstein quote that says, "The definition of *insanity* is *doing the same thing* over and over again and expecting different results."

What's crazy is that many entrepreneurs recognize that there's increasing competition in their industries, but they keep doing the same things and fail to innovate their business models.

To stay competitive, you need to learn new skills and try new things on an ongoing basis. This is especially true as technology becomes a bigger and bigger part of our daily lives and businesses. While foundational business principles change very little over the years, when it comes to technology, what was cutting edge yesterday is outdated today.

One of the best ways to stand out among the competition is to keep your skills up to date.

While it might seem overwhelming at times, it is possible to stay on top of new trends without wasting too much time. The trick is to develop the habit of focusing on lifelong learning and continuous improvement.

In this section, we'll look at the following habits to make this happen:

- ESH #17: Maximize dead time
- ESH #18: Read 30 minutes a day
- ESH #19: Develop new skills

- ESH #20: Capture ideas

ESH #17: Maximize "Dead Time"

Static businesses are dying businesses. Owners who don't keep up with industry changes often lose out to companies that use innovative business models. That's why it's important to embrace lifelong learning and focus on continuous improvement.

We'll admit it's often hard to find time to stay on the cutting edge and learn new skills.

The good news is that there are pockets of "dead time" throughout the day. You know, those times of day that are wasted on mindless activities. Some are just a few minutes long, while others may be as much as 15 minutes or more. You can accomplish a lot during these snippets of time to move your business forward.

Before we go further, let's acknowledge that we all need alone time to think, meditate and simply relax. We're not talking about multitasking, which we've already mentioned is a very ineffective way to work. To be clear, we're not talking about living like you're some kind of machine that never takes a break.

However, there is great benefit to taking advantage of dead time.

Here are a few examples:

Driving is an excellent time to listen to educational audio books, podcasts related to your industry or materials that will help you improve in other aspects of your business.

As an entrepreneur, you may feel that you don't have enough time to keep up with new information. Fortunately, modern cars come equipped with the technology you need to stream podcasts directly from your cellphone. This can easily turn your driving time into educational time.

A great tool for this is the Stitcher app (http://www.stitcher.com/), which streams podcasts, radio shows and live radio stations. It's also compatible with both the iPhone and Android platforms. Stitcher is Steve's educational tool of choice; he uses this app to listen to more than 20 shows on a weekly basis.

Cooking is another mindless activity that lends itself well to learning time. Rebecca often has her phone or computer on the kitchen counter when she's cooking. During this time, she listens to podcasts, watches webinars and checks out educational video content.

If you're concerned about your electronics getting wet or having food spill on them while you cook, consider buying a wall mount for your device. Then install it on the wall above the counter where you do your food prep.

When someone else is doing the driving (or flying), you can read, write and listen to podcasts or videos stored on your device. If the flight you're on has Wi-Fi, you can use the travel time to catch up on emails, plan out projects and brainstorm new business ideas.

5 Helpful Educational Tools

You can maximize dead time with five educational tools:

#1. Smartphones

Smartphones are probably one of the best all-purpose tools when it comes to maximizing dead time. These devices are great because you can access all kinds of content and you're likely to carry the phone with you most of the time. It's also the central hub for accessing the four other tools listed below.

#2. Task list apps

We've already talked about the importance of making project lists. One place to store them is in a task list app, like Evernote (http://www.evernote.com/) or Remember the Milk (http://rememberthemilk.com/). During dead time, pull out your list and complete little tasks that are important but not urgent.

If you prefer an old-fashioned method, jot down tasks on an index card and keep the card in your wallet or purse.

#3. Podcast apps

We've already talked about Stitcher, but let me talk about a side benefit of using podcast apps. Most apps let you subscribe to and download your favorite podcasts to your phone so you always have something to listen to—even if you're somewhere without an Internet connection.

#4. Kindle app

You might be reading this book on some type of Kindle app. If not, you probably know that the Kindle app makes it easy to read books on almost any device. By using the app, you will always be able to access reading material even if you don't have your Kindle with you or your Kindle battery dies.

#5: Online courses

You can learn pretty much anything on sites like Udemy (https://www.udemy.com/), Lynda.com (http://www.lynda.com/) and Skillshare (http://www.skillshare.com/). If you need to grow your business in one area, then you can easily find someone to teach you on one of these sites.

IMPLEMENTATION

Want to make best use of dead time? Here's a simple action plan for getting started:

Action 1: Over the course of the next week, make a list of all of the dead time that occurs. Think carefully about those small blocks (five to ten minutes each) when you normally waste time playing Candy Crush.

Action 2: Create a plan for using that dead time effectively. Install apps on your phone to access educational material when you're out and about, download podcasts, add books to your Kindle app and bookmark industry-related articles.

Action 3: Set goals for what you'll accomplish during dead time. For instance, you may set a goal of listening to one book per week or listening to a certain number of podcasts per week. Setting a goal can motivate you to get in the habit of using your dead time effectively.

ESH #18: Read 30 Minutes a Day

It should come as no surprise that reading leads to academic success, but reading is also linked to professional success.

President Harry S. Truman has been quoted as saying, "Not all readers are leaders, but all leaders are readers," and W. Fusselman said, "Today a reader, tomorrow a leader."

While there's no guarantee that reading 30 minutes per day will make you a leader in your industry, doing so certainly increases your odds. If you choose not to be an active reader, you can get along in your business okay, but you may find yourself stuck one day and unable to grow beyond your current level.

Reading Habits of Average People vs. Reading Habits of Successful Entrepreneurs

The average person reads only one book per year, with 60 percent only getting through the first chapter. In contrast, CEOs of Fortune 500 companies read an average of four to five books per month (http://normadoiron.net/consecrate-yourself-fully-to-the-entrepreneurship-opportunity/), with some reading as many as a book a day.

While there are many factors that contribute to income level, active readers make five times more money (http://normadoiron.net/consecrate-yourself-fully-to-the-entrepreneurship-opportunity/) than non-readers, so if you want to boost the amount of money you make, then developing the reading habit won't hurt!

Your Goal: Read 30 Minutes per Day

As a busy entrepreneur, you may feel like you don't have time to read, but the good news is that you can accomplish a lot by reading just 30 minutes per day.

According to a Forbes article (http://www.forbes.com/sites/brettnelson/2012/06/04/do-you-read-fast-enough-to-be-successful/), the average adult reads

300 words per minute, the average high-level executive reads 575 words per minute, and speed readers read 1500 words per minute.

Now let's say you're an average person who never goes beyond 300 words per minute. At 30 minutes per day, you can complete a 50,000-word book (approximately 200 pages) in 5.55 days, which will allow you to comfortably read one book per week.

One thing to keep in mind is that you don't have to do it all at once; you can read in 10-minute chunks three times per day or perhaps start and end your day with 15 minutes of reading. Use dead time to get more reading done each day (ESH #17).

Don't Like to Read?

There are audio versions of most books, so if reading is something you don't enjoy, try audiobooks.

Rebecca's husband likes to read, but he is a slow reader so he checks out many audiobooks from the library. This helps him "read" more books than he otherwise could.

If you prefer to buy audiobooks, an Audible (http://www.audible.com/) subscription is your best bet. Audible has a large selection of fiction and nonfiction titles. Kindle books are also text-to-speech enabled, so you can listen to most titles if you don't feel like reading.

It's important to note that the text-to-speech function is computer-generated audio that sounds robotic. For the best listening experience, purchase an audio version narrated by an actual person. Trust us—listening to a robot voice can get very boring, very quickly.

Walt Disney said, "There is more treasure in books than in all the pirate's loot on Treasure Island." If you want to vastly enrich your life and business, give reading 30 minutes per day a try.

IMPLEMENTATION

Ready to develop the reading habit? Here are a few action steps for getting started:

Action 1: Commit to the 30-minute reading habit on a daily basis. Stay accountable by signing up for a free service like Lift.do (https://www.lift.do/plans/1796-read-30-minutes).

Action 2: Carry a book with you at all times (or use the Kindle app on your smartphone or tablet) so that you can read when you have downtime.

Here are some nonfiction ideas that might help you grow your business: profiles of successful companies, profiles of successful individuals, books that teach a professional skill and anything that relates to marketing.

Action 3: Don't fall into the trap of sticking just to your market. Great ideas come from learning from people in different sectors and applying their strategies to your business. (A great resource is the Entrepreneur on Fire, http://www.entrepreneuronfire.com/, podcast where John Lee Dumas connects with successful business owners from a wide variety of industries.)

Action 4: Gather information on audio versions of books. For example, look into an Audible subscription, check with libraries in your area to see what audio book options are available and subscribe to podcasts.

Action 5: Pick an area that you want to grow in and read three or more books in that area. One book will lay the foundation, the second book will help you to build on the foundation and the third book will help you to internalize the information. You'll find that the more you read about a particular topic, the more you'll internalize the information and turn it into a core part of your thinking.

ESH #19: Develop New Skills

If your business is stagnating, it could be that you have stopped learning and growing. The world around us is changing at a rapid pace. While what you did in the past worked well, it may no longer be enough to stand out from the competition. If you don't continuously learn new skills, you probably won't enjoy continued success in your business.

Reading 30 minutes per day is, of course, an excellent foundation. It gives you the knowledge you need to be at the top of your field. But knowledge is only one piece of the puzzle. Knowledge without skills won't get you very far because skills are what allow you to actually take action on what you know.

Chad Hugghins of FlourMillMedia (http://www.flourmillmedia.com/) writes, "The one habit that consistently helps me better my business is the daily habit of setting time aside to learn. Social media and video marketing is constantly changing, and it's vital to stay up to date with best practices, technologies and strategies.

"I use an app called Pocket (https://getpocket.com/), including their Chrome plugin, to save articles and videos throughout the day. I then use at least 30 minutes, usually after lunch, to read, learn and be inspired. This keeps our services cutting edge and keeps us motivated to stay ahead of the curve."

Likewise, marketer Simon Tam (http://simontam.biz/) says, "One habit that I have is to set up a daily, consistent time for me to engage in building skills. This might be learning a new program, practicing a different language or expanding an existing skill that I have.

"The daily habit of learning and challenging the mind keeps thinking processes clear. It allows me to build a more robust skill set that I can use to enhance my business. The mind, like the body, needs a variety of different types of exercises to keep it fit. When it is stretched and challenged, it handles stress and complex problems much more efficiently and effectively."

Expose Yourself to New Things

It's important to expose yourself to new things on a regular basis, even if you don't see an immediate application. You never know when a new skill or experience will be applicable in another aspect of life or make something else easier for you in the future.

Rebecca and her family spent six months in India working as cultural researchers. While it may seem that the time she spent in India has absolutely nothing to do with what she currently does, it helped equip her for many other aspects of life and business.

For example, while in India, she had to make herself hit the streets to find people to interview. As an introvert, it wasn't always easy to do that, but the situation pushed her to learn how to initiate conversations with strangers. That skill has made it easier for her to interact with people at conferences and networking events. If she can push herself to interact with people in a foreign country who may not even speak English, she can certainly go up to a stranger at a conference and start a conversation.

How to Overcome Fear

Fear is one of the biggest hindrances to learning new things. When Rebecca's family arrived in India, her supervisor gave just one assignment on the first day: Get on some type of public transportation, get lost and then find your way back home.

This was a very important first assignment because it caused every team member to immediately face and overcome their fears so that they could then go out and do their jobs.

In the course of running your business, you don't have to get lost in a foreign country, but you will have to overcome fears associated with learning new things.

For instance, there may be new technologies that you have to learn, and you may not be technologically inclined. Or you may need to learn public speaking, when the thought of getting in front of an audience terrifies you.

Regardless of what skills you need to learn, if you want to grow to your maximum potential, there will be times when you have to do things that frighten you a bit. The best way to overcome those fears is to simply do them sooner rather than later.

Just in Time Learning

While facing your fears sooner rather than later is a good thing, there is also a lot to be said for learning things "just in time." Just in time is a business concept that originated in Japan in the 1950s and was adopted by Toyota and other Japanese companies.

Toyota applied the concept by ordering the inventory needed to build their cars "just in time." This increased their bottom line because they didn't need to spend money sooner than needed. Since they had less inventory, they didn't need as much warehouse space. Using this approach also helped Toyota increase productivity as a result of wasting less.

This same principle can be applied to learning. For example, there's no need to learn skills that you may not apply at some point in the future. That will only waste your time because you may not ever end up using the skill. And even if you do need it, you might be forced to relearn it if you've forgotten how to do it.

Learning things you don't really need to know can also be a form of procrastination since it's more comfortable to learn instead of taking action.

Using a "just in time" approach to learning wastes less time and increases productivity.

Use What You Already Have

Many entrepreneurs are in the habit of buying the latest, greatest shiny object. While purchasing "how to" programs is an important aspect of learning new skills, you waste money (and time) if you fail to take action. You need to take the time to go through the material and apply the information before rushing out to buy the next big thing.

The secret to success isn't buying the latest product—it's knowing where you need to grow, getting actionable information and taking immediate action.

Make Learning a Way of Life

Unless you're intentional about it, it's easy to get stuck in a rut and let your skills atrophy. To keep things fresh, make the following activities a normal part of your everyday life:

- Meet people
- Talk to strangers
- Travel
- Get out of your house
- Try new things
- Enroll in courses

The more new ideas you're exposed to, the more opportunities you'll have to grow your business.

IMPLEMENTATION

The following is a simple action plan to improve your skills and stand out from the competition:

Action 1: Stay on top of the trends that are most important for your market. A simple way to do this is to use Google Alerts (https://www.google.com/alerts), a service that compiles relevant news articles based on specific search parameters. You can set it up so that the results are sent to you in a daily email digest. Review the email in the morning or during a break in between tasks as a way of staying on top of what's going on in your industry.

Action 2: Enroll in online classes related to the next skill you'd like to develop (remember the importance of "just in time" learning). Some great options for this are Skillshare (http://skillshare.com/), Udemy (http://udemy.com/) and Lynda.com (http://lynda.com/).

Action 3: Block out time on your calendar for learning. Having designated time for learning new skills will help learning become a habit.

Action 4: Add specific learning tasks to your task list. For instance, if you have an online course you want to go through, create tasks, with due dates, for going through the different modules. Take these tasks and turn them into a project list (ESH #9).

Action 5: Hire a mentor. Find someone who really knows what they're doing and pay their rate for a few quick strategy sessions. Use a site like Clarity.fm (https://clarity.fm/) to find experts who possess particular skills.

ESH #20: Capture Ideas

If you've been implementing the habits presented thus far in this book, there's a good chance your mind is bursting with new ideas.

The bottom line is we're all constantly bombarded with ideas. The best ideas seem to come from out of nowhere, often while doing mindless tasks such as exercising, finishing household chores, showering or even sleeping. You probably have no shortage of ideas that could lead to great success in your business.

That's the good news. The bad news is that as quickly as ideas come, they go, and many good ideas are lost if they aren't captured in some way.

Additionally, according to the Zeigarnick Effect, any incomplete thought—such as an idea or task you need to complete—will occupy your mind until you take some kind of action on it by either completing the task or capturing the idea with a plan for accomplishing the task.

The ideas that bounce around in your mind can prevent you from focusing completely on your current tasks. In a sense, they will nag you until you do something with them.

The solution is to make it a habit to capture every idea—the moment they pop into your head. This will free up your mind to work on your present tasks without interruption. You'll also build a rich database of ideas for products, offline marketing campaigns and other important aspects of your business.

It may seem silly to write down every little idea, but practicing this habit on a daily basis clears your mind and ensures you always have new strategies for growing the business.

Here are some ways to capture ideas:

** Go low-tech and use pen and paper. Carry around a little notebook with you at all times. This way, any time an idea pops into your head, you have a place to write it down.

** Evernote is a popular high-tech option for capturing ideas. A free version is available for Macs and PCs, and smartphone apps are available as well.

The great thing about Evernote is that you can use it to capture your ideas in several different formats: voice recordings, photos, typed notes and Web clippings. Then you can organize them in a logical way that makes it easy to find your ideas again.

**Outlook has a Notes application where you can jot down your ideas and assign them to different categories, contacts, etc. This is a good option if you use Outlook to manage your email, calendar and tasks.

** Some people prefer the hybrid approach of using a notepad and pen or smartphone to capture ideas when out and about. Then they transfer their ideas to a high-tech system once they are back in front of a computer.

Regardless of which system you use, the key is to use it consistently and make sure all of your ideas are captured in a central location.

IMPLEMENTATION

It's not that hard to form the habit of capturing ideas. Simply implement the following action plan:

Action 1: Pick your preferred method for capturing and organizing ideas. You may need to experiment to find out what works best for you. The important thing to remember is that any of the above options will work, so don't agonize over which one is best.

If you're having a hard time deciding, pick up a notebook that is small enough to carry with you at all times and start using it. You can always go to a more elaborate system later.

Action 2: Get into the habit of jotting down every single idea that pops into your head. Don't assume you'll remember later on. Just write it down as soon as possible.

Action 3: Go through your ideas on a weekly basis. If they are unorganized, then this is the time to put them into a logical order. Determine which ideas you want to take action on soon, in the next quarter, in six months or "someday."

Action 4: Create a project plan for the ideas you want to implement immediately. Identify the first steps, schedule them into your calendar and get started.

Action 5: Schedule time to review the ideas you want to take action on sometime beyond the next quarter so you don't forget them.

Challenge #4: Poor Business Relationships

You can only go so far in business on your own. In fact, it's almost impossible to succeed if you have poor relationships with customers and the people on your team. And even if *you* have great relationships, if your business location is a toxic work environment, then it's on the pathway toward failure

The truth is that many entrepreneurs fail because they don't invest enough in developing healthy teams and fail to deal with problems as they arise.

In this section, we'll talk about specific interpersonal habits you can develop to improve the relationships you have with employees, customers and other people in your industry.

In this section we'll look at the following habits:

- ESH #21: Network and build connections
- ESH #22: Keep your promises
- ESH #23: Embrace the power of no
- ESH #24: Be a leader, not a micromanager
- ESH #25: Know how to speak
- ESH #26: Know how to listen

ESH #21: Network and Build Connections

Entrepreneurship requires a great deal of self-discipline, but the entrepreneurs who put too much emphasis on the word "self" have a hard time making it.

While we're each ultimately responsible for getting up every day and doing the necessary work, that isn't enough. None of us can make it without the help of others and a willingness to receive this support.

Here are a few ways to build important connections:

#1. Join a Mastermind Group

Both Steve and Rebecca are in mastermind groups that are instrumental to their success.

An important aspect of mastermind groups is that they are built on the foundation of both giving and receiving. For example, members of a mastermind group may help you promote your products or services, and you may provide assistance to others in your areas of expertise.

Mastermind meetings are also a great place to let your guard down and share both the struggles and victories in your business. They provide a safe environment in which to be real about what is happening in your professional life. What you often get back is encouragement, input and, when needed, a swift kick in the pants.

#2. Attend Live Networking Events

Even if you have a home-based business, as both Rebecca and Steve do, it's still important to attend live events. You never know whom you might meet at one of those events.

For example, this book would have never been written if it wasn't for the fact that Rebecca traveled from her home in Colorado and Steve traveled from his home in New Jersey to the event in San Diego where they met.

They kept in touch and, several months after their initial meeting, decided to work together on this book. That connection wouldn't have happened had they stayed in the comfort zone of their own homes.

When you network, you lay the foundation for gaining mentors, investors, customers, advisors, employees and even partners, as was the case with Steve and Rebecca.

You can definitely accomplish more when you have a solid network in place than you could ever accomplish on your own.

#3. Have an Attitude of Serving

One mistake many people make when it comes to networking is looking for people who can help them, instead of focusing on helping others. Naturally, you want to make beneficial connections when you attend a networking event, but if you go into relationships looking for what people can do for you, your networking efforts won't go very far.

Instead, always be on the lookout for opportunities to assist people. Rebecca would even go so far as to say pay attention to those little nudges to reach out to someone.

She did just that a few years back, and it totally changed the course of her life and business.

At the time, she was working a full-time job but wanted to quit and start her own business. She somehow got on the email list of Facebook marketing expert Amy Porterfield. On one of Amy's sales pages, Rebecca noticed a pretty big mistake. Although she wasn't sure that her feedback would be welcomed, she reached out to Amy to let her know.

As she was writing the email to Amy, she felt the urge to offer to do 50 pages of proofreading for her for free, with no strings attached.

Amy decided to take Rebecca up on her offer, but, to help make it worth Rebecca's time, she offered to do a personalized Facebook strategy guide in exchange for the proofreading. They got on the phone together. During the conversation, Amy asked questions that gave Rebecca an opportunity to share about her passions and skills.

You can imagine how surprised Rebecca was when, by the end of the conversation, Amy said, "I'll be your first client." While the thought of working for Amy had never crossed Rebecca's mind, it just so happened that Amy was looking to hire a new team member and Rebecca's skillset fit perfectly with what she needed.

Three weeks later, Rebecca started working for Amy. Five months later, she quit her job to run her new business. She worked for Amy for three years until she recently transitioned into writing full-time.

Rebecca had no ulterior motive in reaching out to Amy and offering to do the proofreading for free. She simply wanted to help. But that simple action set off a series of events that laid the foundation for the solid business she enjoys today.

#4. Focus on Quality over Quantity

To some degree, quantity is important. It's hard to get very far with only a few people in your network. At the same time, having hundreds or even thousands of people in your network who aren't a good fit does very little for your business. Instead, focus on quality connections and gradually build the numbers over time.

IMPLEMENTATION

You can build connections by doing the following:

Action 1: Do (at least) one thing every day to grow and strengthen your network. For instance, you might want to call or email a person in your industry. The key is to spend a little bit of time doing this *every day* rather than spending big chunks of time on it sporadically. Commit to networking—meeting and helping new people as well as following up and developing those relationships over time.

Action 2: Look for opportunities to help others. When talking to someone in your industry, find out how you can help them without asking anything in return.

Action 3: Consider joining a mastermind group so you'll have a solid group of people you can be transparent with as you build your business.

Action 4: Join Facebook or LinkedIn groups and provide value to other members. Rather than joining several groups all at once, pick a few and work on developing relationships in those groups.

If you don't connect well in one group, join another and see if you mesh well with those members. While you might try several groups to find a good fit, avoid bouncing from one group to the next without taking the time to truly cultivate relationships.

Action 5: Meet people in a live setting. Have breakfast or lunch with a colleague or friend at least once a week. Attend activities such as Chamber of Commerce events, "Meet Ups" (from Meetup.com) and market-specific conferences.

ESH #22: Keep Your Promises

Richard Branson has been quoted as saying, "Your brand is only as good as your reputation." It's true; you can have the best product or service on the planet, but if you have a bad reputation, you'll have a hard time selling it.

One of the best ways to maintain a positive reputation is to always keep your promises.

While it takes time to build a good reputation with your peers, customers and people of influence in your industry, that good reputation can be lost in a moment if you break your promises.

Because of this, it's vitally important to stick to every promise you make. Failure to do so can have a negative snowball effect on your organization.

What's a simple way to show everyone that you keep your promises?

It's simple…

…Show up on time.

When you show up to appointments late, people will make snap judgments about you as a person. If you stroll in 10 minutes late, you might lose business or tick off a potential customer.

The bottom line is that when you agree to meet someone at a certain time, you are promising to be there at that specific time—even if you don't say, "I promise to be there on time." The promise is implied when you make the appointment. This is true for phone, online and in-person appointments.

Failure to show up on time is a sign of disrespect. Renowned direct marketer Dan Kennedy says that punctuality is his #1 habit for success (http://entrepreneur.com/article/230107). He even goes as far as to link respect for others' time with respect for others' opinions, property, rights, agreements and contracts. In his words, it's as simple as "being where you're supposed to be when you're supposed to be there, as promised, without exception, without excuse, every time, all the time."

Steve has a very similar belief. Recently, he decided to not do business with someone because the guy blew him off for a scheduled interview and came back a <u>month</u> later with a weak excuse for his no-show. Now all of his emails automatically go to the trash folder in Steve's inbox.

You might think this is extreme, but you'll find that when you don't respect other people's time, the doors of opportunity will quickly shut in your face.

As an entrepreneur, you'll often have in-person meetings. As a general rule, you always want to allow more than enough time to drive to a meeting. This is especially important when going to a new, unfamiliar location. Actually, even if you know where the meeting place is located, it's best to add extra time to compensate for any potential problems (like getting stuck in traffic) that may occur on the way.

If you arrive at your destination well in advance, you can stop at a coffee shop near your meeting location and use the extra time to review notes for your meeting, or catch up on email or some other task.

Overall, it's not hard to keep your promises. Just think carefully about what you're agreeing to, say no when a project doesn't match your goals and do everything you can to follow through with a commitment.

IMPLEMENTATION

You can develop the positive habit of keeping your promises by doing each of the following:

Action 1: Think carefully before agreeing to commitments. Even go as far as saying "no" if you're not 100 percent sure you can follow through. (We'll talk more about this in the next section.) Honestly, it's better to commit to fewer obligations than it is to make weak promises that often fall through.

Action 2: Create a habit of showing up on time for everything. When you have a meeting or conversation scheduled, allow at least 15 minutes of buffer time in case an unexpected event comes up.

Action 3: If you fail to keep a promise, then own up to it. Be quick to apologize and don't make excuses. In these situations, it can also help to analyze why you failed to keep the promise so that you can fix the underlying issue and never do it again.

ESH #23: Embrace the Power of "No"

In the previous chapter, we talked about the importance of keeping promises.

While there are many underlying causes of broken promises, one of the biggest is saying yes to things when you should have said no.

Saying yes when a "no" response is more appropriate leads to an overloaded schedule where things fall through the cracks. In other cases, you may say yes to things that you really don't want to do, so you end up procrastinating or doing a bad job.

An important thing to keep in mind is that "no" doesn't have to be a dirty word. It can even be a way of showing respect to the other person, especially if there is a chance you won't do a good job on the task if you say yes.

Here are a few ways to say no while still maintaining positive business relationships:

#1. Don't be a people pleaser.

If you have a problem with saying no, it could be that you're a people pleaser and simply don't want to let people down. Perhaps you don't want to disappoint anyone, or maybe you're scared that they won't like you.

What's interesting is that you're more likely to disappoint people if you're doing things you shouldn't be doing. You might not do a good job or, even worse, you may drop the ball and let the person down. These actions can be much more damaging than saying no from the very beginning.

#2. Be firm with "button pushers."

Something to be aware of is that some people know how to push buttons and make you feel guilty when you say no.

For example, they may pout or tell you how disappointed they are that you can't (or won't) do what they've asked. They may even say things like, "I was really counting on you to do this."

While it's okay to carefully reconsider requests, be mindful of whether or not you're being manipulated. This is especially true if you have an ongoing relationship with the person and there is a pattern of manipulation.

#3. Determine your priorities.

One of the best ways to evaluate a request is to look at your long-term goals (ESH #10), then filter the request to see whether or not it fits your goals.

Keep in mind that at least one of your goals should be focused on others. For example, if you're becoming a leader in your industry, you may get requests for mentoring, interviews and so on from those who are just starting out. If you want to be a true leader, you may need to provide your expertise to others for free, on a limited basis.

The key is to make sure that you say yes to the most important things first and block out time in a way that helps you accomplish your priorities.

Saying no doesn't make you a selfish person. In fact, it can make you a generous person since saying no to the wrong things opens up time to say *yes* to the right things. Remember that whenever you agree to one thing, you are, in essence, saying no to something else that might be more important.

#4. Get out of previous agreements.

If you make a habit of doing what is written about in this chapter, it should be very rare that you'll say yes to something when you should have said no. However, if that does happen, there are a few ways to deal with it.

If it's a one-time commitment, you should probably just do it and learn from your mistake instead of breaking your promise.

If the commitment is an ongoing one, then it's best to bow out of it as gracefully as you can, as soon as you possibly can.

For instance, one big mistake Rebecca made early in her business was working with certain clients who weren't a good fit. She spent more than a year working with one client who caused her unnecessary stress. The bad thing is, he represented approximately 40 percent of her income, so she felt trapped in the relationship.

When she finally quit, she received an opportunity from another client that she didn't feel good about, but, due to her big loss of income, she said yes even though her gut was telling her to say no.

In this case, however, she declined the new offer the very next day instead of staying in a situation that didn't feel right. Obviously, she did it with a great deal of apology and tact, letting the client know that, after sleeping on it, she felt she wasn't right for the position. She went on to recommend some other people who would perhaps be a good fit.

While it would have been better if Rebecca had said no in the first place, quickly apologizing and backing out of the commitment was a better option than being in a bad situation for a number of months.

IMPLEMENTATION

How do you turn the art of saying no into a regular habit?

Here are a few ideas for getting started:

Action 1: Identify your business and personal goals. Review these on a daily basis so you instinctively know what offers are the right fit.

Action 2: Block out time on your calendar that relates to your business goals. It's also important to schedule time for vacations, family time and fun activities. This will help you develop a clearer picture of how little free time you may have.

Action 3: Avoid immediately saying yes to a request. Instead, promise to get back to someone about their request within a week. If you immediately know there is no way you'll say yes, don't string the person along. Just be straightforward and direct.

Before you say yes to a request, consider whether or not it fits with your goals. Also take a look at your calendar to see whether you have time to complete the request to the best of your abilities. If so, go ahead and pencil in time to work on it. If there's not a slot for it on your calendar, your answer should be no by default.

ESH #24: Be a Leader, Not a Micromanager

Even if you're a solopreneur, you'll need to add people to your team at some point to grow your business. *How* you relate to these people will go a long way toward your entrepreneurial success (or failure).

One of the worst things you can do is micromanage your team members. While team members *may* value your input, giving valuable feedback is a very different animal than micromanaging.

For example, on this book project, both Steve and Rebecca had specific tasks to accomplish. While they exchanged frequent updates (and asked questions when needed), they trusted each other to "own" their assigned project tasks.

Ultimately, this made for a much more positive working relationship than if Steve had micromanaged Rebecca and expected a report every day on what she had accomplished.

The Difference Between a Boss and a Leader

A boss is in charge on the basis of the authority he or she possesses. For instance, a boss may be the business owner and the one who pays the bills. He—or she—who pays the bills often makes the rules.

In contrast, a leader inspires and encourages team members and, because of that, gets the best work from subordinates.

You can make this happen by assigning tasks that fit the individual strengths of team members with clear expectations about what's needed. Start by giving words of encouragement and affirmation. Clear up any confusion on the project and encourage team members to contact you if they get stuck. Then let them get to work!

Give Proven Team Members Even More Leeway

Newer team members may need to check in on a frequent basis, so there's nothing wrong with establishing a few checkpoints along the way. This doesn't mean that you need to know every detail. Just give deadlines for the parts of a big project and regularly check in to make sure things are moving forward.

Once team members have proven themselves, these checkpoints become unnecessary unless there is a critical milestone required by the client.

Whatever you do, don't practice behaviors that send a message of distrust to team members. For example, one of Rebecca's former clients had his assistant ask Rebecca if she was going to get tasks done on time. This was after she had been working for him for several months and never missed a deadline.

This was a demoralizing thing for him to do, especially since her previous actions proved her reliability. While her manners (not to mention not wanting to tick him off) kept Rebecca from mouthing off, she felt like saying, "Look, I've never missed a deadline before. Why do you keep having your assistant ask if I'm going to get things done on time?"

As the demand for Rebecca's services grew, she evaluated which clients caused her the most stress and stopped working for the person who, in spite of her proven track record, had his assistant check up on her regularly.

The bottom line is that you should only distrust team members who have given you a reason to distrust them and give all other team members the benefit of the doubt.

Encourage Independence and Creativity

If you really want your team members to excel, encourage them to be independent and reward them for creativity.

For instance, if they take action on a matter but do it differently than you would have, commend them for being proactive. Then (if needed) gently guide them in a way that will encourage them to make the necessary tweaks. In essence, you're empowering team members to try new things—even if they make mistakes.

For example, Rebecca has worked with many clients who travel internationally, and sometimes she needs to make executive decisions on time-sensitive matters when her clients can't be reached. When her clients return, she updates them on what happened. In the best-case scenario, they are pleased.

On the few occasions they would have done something differently, they commend her for taking action and then let her know what they would have done had they been present.

That behavior gives her freedom to use her best judgment without fear since she knows she won't be in trouble for taking action. It also serves as a good training opportunity so that she'll be even better equipped to handle situations in the future.

Audrey Darrow, President of Earth Source Organics (http://www.righteouslyrawchocolate.com/), has the right idea. She writes, "I make sure my employees' energy is in line with my energy and my vision. This means that I come to work with enthusiasm and a positive attitude and give kudos to my employees everyday. This helps them to stay positive and maintain a high level of energy, which helps us attract sales. If my employees know and understand my vision, then they get excited because they know they will make money before I do!"

Provide Rewards for Good Ideas

When Rebecca's husband was in the Army, he submitted an idea for how his unit could go paperless. That was an innovative idea at the time and would save the unit a lot of money. His idea was not only listened to, it was implemented. He received public recognition and a hefty check based on a percentage of the estimated savings. You can bet that when his colleagues saw him praised and witnessed the check presentation, they saw the value of submitting good ideas.

Your budget may not permit you to cut a check whenever a team member presents a good idea, but it's important to listen carefully to what they're telling you. Express appreciation for ideas and, when it makes sense to do so, implement them and give credit where credit is due. This will motivate people to come up with creative solutions to your business problems. You never know how much profit an idea from someone on your team may generate!

IMPLEMENTATION

Want to be a true leader of your business?

Below are a few strategies for empowering team members to do great work:

Action 1: Until a team member has proven otherwise, give them the benefit of the doubt when it comes to trusting that they are doing what you've assigned them.

Action 2: Be a positive leader who creates a vibrant work environment. Consider developing a reward system that encourages your team members to share ideas.

Also, praise people in public for a job well done. If a mistake is made, avoid the "blame game." Instead, have a private one-on-one conversation about what needs to be fixed and what to do in the future.

Action 3: If you tend to micromanage, admit it to your team members and apologize when needed. Let your team know of your commitment to do a better job in that area, and then stick to it.

ESH #25: Know How to Speak

Many times people are judged on the basis of how they speak.

If you're articulate, you'll be deemed to be trustworthy and on top of things. In contrast, if you stumble over your words, hesitate and communicate poorly, people will be less likely to feel that you know what you're talking about.

This may seem unfair, especially since it's possible to be very good at what you do even if you don't have good speaking skills. Whether it's fair or not, people will judge you based solely on your speaking ability. That means that, if you want your business to grow, this is an area you can't afford to neglect.

As an entrepreneur, you're in sales even if you don't consider yourself to be a salesperson. For example, you have to be able to talk to others convincingly about your product or service so that they see the value of your offer. You may also need to negotiate, and if you come across as lacking in confidence, it will be hard to get the best deal.

Establishing Yourself as an Expert

When you speak with uncertainty, people have less confidence in the value of your message. Expertise doesn't matter if you're unable to convince people that you *actually* know your stuff. The simplest solution? Know how to talk like an expert.

For example, Rebecca recently went for a physical, and she came away from it feeling very uncertain about the doctor's expertise because of the way he spoke. Instead of being confident and communicating clearly, he often looked down, hesitated and deferred to her opinion on things.

It's possible that Rebecca's doctor is very knowledgeable, but, due to the way he spoke, she's thinking she may need to find a new doctor who knows what he's doing.

Practice Make Perfect

Not everyone is born a speaker; in fact, most people struggle with it. You've probably heard that speaking is the number one fear and that many people would rather die or suffer some other tragedy than speak in front of others.

You may find public speaking difficult. You may not be very good at it right now, but one thing is certain—you can get better with practice.

Rebecca has always been very shy. From elementary school through high school, she avoided giving speeches and seldom spoke up in class.

This all changed for her in college. She attended a small private college that required students to do a lot of speaking. The class sizes were small, and the other students were encouraging, so little by little she gained confidence and actually began to enjoy public speaking.

IMPLEMENTATION

Want to practice and improve your public speaking skills? Here are a few ways to get started:

Action 1: Attend networking events and conferences. These are great places to use your elevator pitch and practice conversing with people.

At networking events, you probably won't have to get up on stage, but you'll have an opportunity to speak to people one-on-one or in small groups. Since you'll often answer many of the same questions over and over again, these conversations offer a great opportunity to practice communicating with others.

Action 2: Join Toastmasters or take a public speaking class. These classes are typically offered at local business centers or nearby community colleges. Participating in these activities will put you in a situation where you have to speak and get direct feedback on your performance.

Action 3: Look for opportunities to get interviewed on podcasts. Rebecca prefers to get the questions she'll be asked ahead of time so she can better prepare and feel more confident in her responses. Steve prefers to talk "off the cuff" because most of the questions deal directly with strategies he implements on a daily basis.

We both have our own personal preferences, but the important thing is that we use these interviews to improve our communication skills.

You can also start your own podcast as a way to get more practice. Whether you have a solo show, a partnership or a show featuring your interviews with other people, you'll have to speak on a regular basis to create a compelling show. To learn more, check out this free tutorial (created by Pat Flynn) on how to start a podcast (http://www.smartpassiveincome.com/how-to-start-a-podcast-podcasting-tutorial/).

Action 4: Write an "elevator pitch" for your business. An elevator pitch is a summary of your business that can be given in the amount of time it takes to ride an elevator. Practice it so that when people ask you what you do, you'll be able to articulate it well.

This is a useful strategy for in-person networking events. Having a memorized spiel about you and your business makes it easy to break the ice and get the conversation rolling.

ESH #26: Know How to Listen

Speaking is just one half of the communication process. While it's *important*, it's often more valuable to pay close attention to what other people are saying.

I'm sure you've encountered people who talk so much that no one else can get a word in edgewise. If you're like everyone else, you start looking for a way to escape as soon as you can.

Don't be the person that causes other people to look for the nearest exist. Practice the habit of active listening instead. Here are two ways to do this:

#1. Learn to ask good questions.

One of the best ways to become a good listener is to focus on the person you're conversing with instead of thinking about what you're going to say next.

To draw the person out, really focus on what they're saying and ask follow-up questions. They don't have to be super insightful or witty, but they should give the person an opportunity to go deeper. You may say something like, "You mentioned xyz. Tell me more about how that works."

#2. Get Feedback

The real power of being a good listener isn't to make you more popular at parties and networking events. It's best used to hear what your customers, prospects and team members are saying.

For instance, you can ask for feedback on your products or services. Then use the feedback to improve the quality of what you're offering.

There are many ways to accomplish this. You can send surveys to your email list to find out what customers want; look at reviews to see what resonates with people in your target audience; and talk with team members about how they'd improve on an existing process.

Don't beat yourself up if you get negative feedback. Even if the feedback seems harsh, look for the kernel of truth in what people are saying and make changes based on this information.

IMPLEMENTATION

Being a good listener doesn't mean that you have to be a pushover. It's more about focusing on others and using the information to make your business more successful. That's why it's important to do the following to improve your "active listening" skills:

Action 1: Give responsive feedback during conversations. Look people in the eye when they speak. Respond to them while they're speaking by nodding, smiling and providing small verbal cues, such as "uh huh," that indicate you're paying attention.

Furthermore, summarize what people say to you to make sure you understood and let them know you were really listening. For instance, you may say something like, "It sounds like xyz was really challenging."

Finally, ask more questions and point the conversation back to the person you're conversing with. If someone asks you a question, answer it and then follow up by asking them a question, providing them with an opportunity to share more about themselves.

Action 2: Regularly ask your customers for feedback. For example, let's say you just landed a new client. After you complete the project, ask how the customer liked it. Then ask if your client has any suggestions for improvement.

Action 3: If you struggle with listening, improve by listening to a short snippet of audio and jotting down what you remember at the end of the clip. Play back the audio and compare it to what you wrote down to see how much you remembered. Not only will this develop your listening skills, it'll also sharpen your memory.

Challenge #5: Stress And Burnout

As we all know, it's not easy to be an entrepreneur. The success of the business rides on your shoulders. If something fails, you can't pass the blame to an incompetent co-worker or boss. The major downside to this reality is that it's easy to quickly burn out from the constant pressure.

We all have moments of stress, but some of them are so overwhelming that you risk losing your passion for running a business. In order to do your best work, you need to focus on living a balanced life.

In this section, we cover the habits that keep the passion alive and help you find that elusive work-life balance:

- ESH #27: Get regular exercise
- ESH #28: Live a healthy lifestyle
- ESH #29: Get a good night's sleep
- ESH #30: Meditate or practice journaling
- ESH #31: Do what you love
- ESH #32: Help others
- ESH #33: Believe in yourself

ESH #27: Get Regular Exercise

Most entrepreneurs find it difficult to get everything done. In fact, if you're like most of us, you often put more hours into your business than you ever did as an employee.

There never seem to be enough hours in the day, and if you're not already exercising, the thought of doing so may make you roll your eyes.

We can certainly understand those feelings, but hang with us here. We'll show you how regular exercise can not only improve your health but also improve your bottom line.

According to the *Journal of Labor Research*, people who exercise earn nine percent more (http://business.time.com/2012/06/08/one-more-reason-to-hit-the-gym-youll-make-more-money/) than those who don't. In fact, there is a correlation between the amount of exercise someone does and their income. In addition, those who exercise on a frequent basis tend to have higher incomes (http://link.springer.com/article/10.1007%2Fs12122-011-9129-2).

In addition to the potential financial benefits, regular exercise can also provide many psychological benefits such as diminished anxiety, higher self-esteem and improved brain function.

If you're out of shape now, the best news of all is that it's never too late to start (http://adviceiq.com/articles/jonathan-deyoe-exercise-success-link). According to the *Journal of Labor Research*, after out of shape employees began exercising, they became more productive and many of them received raises.

These studies were done on employees who don't have as much control over their income. As entrepreneurs, the results can be even more staggering since our income is often directly tied to how much we get done. Since regular exercise is tied to increased productivity, you have even more to gain as an entrepreneur.

Physical and Mental Health Benefits

It should come as no surprise that there are numerous health benefits to exercising, but in addition to increasing the odds of living a long and healthy life, these benefits can make an impact on many aspects of your business.

For example, regular exercise can increase your stamina and concentration. Regardless of your type of business, you need both stamina and concentration. Steve and Rebecca both spend focused time writing every day—the key word being "focused." The more focused we are in our writing, the more words we are able to generate and the better the quality of the writing becomes, which typically leads to more income.

If your business is more physical, having increased stamina and concentration is still a worthwhile outcome of exercise.

If you suffer from depression, you have even more reason to exercise. According to a Harvard study (http://www.health.harvard.edu/newsweek/Exercise-and-Depression-report-excerpt.htm), running a few laps around the block won't do much to aid depression, but a regular exercise program is more effective for relieving depression symptoms than taking medications—with none of the side effects (like weight gain) commonly associated with antidepressants.

Thinking Time

Another great benefit of regular exercise is that it gives you time to think. When Steve is writing a book, he thinks about the book when running. By the time he gets home, he often has many ideas to add to the content. In a way, this regular exercise acts as a distraction-free brainstorming session.

All businesses require thought. There may be important meetings you need to mentally prepare for, problems you need to solve or new products to create. Your exercise time is a great opportunity for coming up with innovative ideas and solutions for your business.

Stress Relief

Running a business can be very stressful, but there are also personal obligations to consider. This is especially true for people who have spouses, children, long-term partners or elderly parents. Exercise can help reduce that stress and give you some much-needed "me time" to disconnect from the pressures of your business.

IMPLEMENTATION

The goal of this chapter isn't to lecture you about the importance of exercise. However, if you're looking to reduce stress and become more productive, you can do so by building a quick exercise routine. Here's an action plan for getting started:

Action 1: Based on your past experiences, choose a type of exercise to focus on. For instance, if you previously liked circuit training but haven't done it recently, circuit training may be a good place to start.

Don't know what exercise to pick?

Our advice is to get started with a walking program.

Walking is a low-cost option you can do no matter where you live. If you live in a place with bad weather, many shopping malls allow early morning walkers. Many gyms and community colleges have indoor tracks, and almost everyone lives near a park.

We generally recommend walking to people starting out because it's the most flexible activity for the stressed-out entrepreneur. All you need is a good pair of walking shoes and a place to go.

Action 2: Explore options at gyms and rec centers in your area. There may be classes, personal trainers and equipment to make exercising more fun and effective.

Action 3: If you have physical conditions that make one form of exercise difficult or inadvisable, don't give up. Instead, consider different types of exercise that may work for you in spite of your limitations. For example, Rebecca loves to walk, but, due to a problem with her feet, she can't do it consistently without it causing her pain. Instead of walking, she works out in a pool at her local rec center.

Action 4: If you have a hard time being consistent, an exercise buddy can help. Having a buddy can enhance your safety, make exercising more fun and help you exercise regularly since someone else is counting on you to show up.

Action 5: Regardless of what type of exercise program you choose, schedule time for it. Without putting it on your calendar, you'll likely never "have time" to do it. Treat this like any other important appointment that you'd never miss. If you make exercise a priority, it will *become* a priority.

ESH #28: Live a Healthy Lifestyle

Exercise is just one part of the equation. While it's a great starting point, you also want to integrate other healthy habits into your life.

The mind and the body are linked together. An unhealthy lifestyle can impact not just your body, but your mind as well, which can have a huge impact on your business.

The great news is that it's not necessary to be an Olympic athlete, a vegan or someone who abstains from alcohol 100 percent of the time. Moderation is key. In fact, allowing yourself an occasional splurge (like a burger, dessert or beer) can help you stick with your health goals for a longer period of time since you know you don't have to abstain for the rest of your life.

When it comes to achieving a healthy balance, you must plan for your indulgences. For instance, you may allow yourself some "cheat meals" on a single weekend day but eat healthy meals the rest of the week. Or you may know that you have a wedding or party to attend and give yourself permission to eat what is served without feeling guilty.

Planning those indulgences can be important because then they aren't really considered "messing up." Therefore, you're less likely to feel that you've failed and give up.

Make Small, Incremental Changes

If you eat a lot of junk food, drink a lot of alcohol or have other unhealthy habits, it's unwise to try to change overnight. Instead, it's best to make one small change at a time.

For example, if you drink a couple of beers a day, cut back to one a day. If you eat nothing but processed foods, start by eating just one piece of fruit or having one green smoothie per day (http://simplegreensmoothies.com/recipes). Once those little changes become more automatic, decrease more of the bad and increase more of the good. You'd be amazed at how much your health can improve by making any of these incremental changes.

IMPLEMENTATION

Action 1: Take a piece of paper and draw a line down the middle. On the left side, write down the things you're currently doing right when it comes to your health. Jot down everything, regardless of how big or small. On the right side, make note of everything you do that is not good for your health.

Action 2: Choose one thing on the left side (a healthy habit) and make a plan to slightly increase it. For instance, if you normally drink one glass of water per day, increase it to two.

Action 3: Choose one thing on the right side (an unhealthy habit) and plan to eliminate or decrease it. For instance, if you're a smoker, you may find it hard to quit altogether, but you can choose to reduce the number of cigarettes you smoke each day.

Action 4: Substitute one bad habit with a related good habit. If you currently drink two soft drinks per day, cut down to one soda and replace the other one with a healthy green smoothie.

You should also determine which indulgences you'll allow, such as pizza on the weekend.

Action 5: On a daily or weekly basis, evaluate how you did when it comes to your health habits. Don't beat yourself up if you mess up. Instead, consider what may have led to the slipup and do what you can to avoid making the same mistake in the future. Keep in mind that every day offers a chance to start fresh!

ESH #29: Get a Full Night's Sleep

Are you proud of being able to work hard on very little sleep? If so, you're in good company. Today's society almost glorifies the practice of being so busy and working so hard that you don't get a good night's sleep.

Coffee drinks are worshipped to the point where many people joke about how they can't survive without their daily caffeine fix. Energy drink consumption has also increased over the years, with more and more people relying on some form of chemical stimulation to keep going.

While there's nothing wrong with enjoying a good cup of coffee, or even the occasional energy drink, there are serious consequences to drinking too many of these beverages— especially energy drinks. For example, according to *Medical News Today* (http://www.medicalnewstoday.com/articles/255078.php), the number of trips to the emergency room as a result of drinking energy drinks doubled between 2007 and 2011.

In addition to caffeine, energy drinks also contain sugar and other chemical additives that make them one of the least healthy drink options out there.

If you're going to pick your poison when it comes to drinks to keep you going, coffee is a better option than energy drinks, but an even better option is to simply get a good night's sleep.

How Much Sleep Do You Need?

We've all heard it said that you need to get eight hours of sleep every night, but everyone is different; some people need more sleep than others, and others need less. It can vary from five hours all the way up to nine hours.

According to a study conducted by the University of California, San Diego (UCSD) School of Medicine (http://health.ucsd.edu/news/2002/02_08_kripke.html), people who sleep only six to seven hours per night have a lower death rate than those who sleep eight hours per night. If you sleep an average of six and a half hours per night, you are probably getting a healthy amount of sleep. Not only will this increase your lifespan, but it'll also help you to stay productive in your waking hours, without resorting to coffee or energy drinks to keep you going.

IMPLEMENTATION

The key to a good night's sleep is to control your environment. You can do this by completing a number of micro-habits that ensure you're going to bed at the right time and preparing for a full night's sleep.

Action 1: Use soothing sounds to block out background noise and lull yourself to sleep. Steve recommends this white noise machine (http://www.developgoodhabits.com/white-noise). You can also use earplugs to block out sound.

Action 2: Get to bed earlier. No doubt about it—getting to bed on time is one of the best ways to get enough sleep. If you get to bed by midnight and get up at 6:00 a.m., you'll get in six hours of sleep. If you go to bed by 10:00 p.m. and rise at 6:00 a.m., you'll get a full eight hours of sleep.

Start by identifying your normal "wake up time," then work your way backward to the ideal bedtime for a great night's sleep. From there, experiment with different times and see how rested you feel in the morning. Eventually you'll discover your optimal amount of sleep.

Action 3: Eliminate smoking, chewing tobacco and drinking alcohol or caffeinated beverages before you go to sleep; all of these substances may keep you awake. You may need to experiment with cutoff times since everyone responds differently to the chemicals in each product.

Action 4: Create a comfortable sleeping environment. Keep your sheets freshly laundered, have a comfortable pillow and invest in linens that help you feel relaxed and comfortable. Adjust the temperature in your room to be "just right."

Temperatures that are too warm or too cold can keep you from sleeping well.

Next, turn off all electronic devices at least 30 minutes before heading to bed and spend that time preparing to sleep. Rebecca has a bedtime routine that includes shutting down her computer, turning off her phone and pampering herself with things like washing and moisturizing her face. This helps her transition from thinking mode to sleep mode.

Finally, use your bedroom exclusively for sleeping and sex. If you have a television in your bedroom, get rid of it. Break the habit of spending time in front of the computer while in bed.

Action 5: Visualize a relaxing scene such as walking on the beach, taking a garden stroll or getting a massage. Discipline yourself to think about relaxing things rather than thinking about your business or other aspects of life that may be troubling.

If you're spiritually inclined, prayer is a good thing to do as you're drifting off to sleep. This is a way to let go of your problems and concerns so that you can sleep without worrying about them.

ESH #30: Meditate or Practice Journaling

Meditation is a discipline practiced in all major religions— and even by non-religious people. The same can be said of journaling. Whether you consider yourself to be religious or not, you can benefit from meditating, journaling or a combination of both.

First, let's look at some of the practices from three different religions that practice meditation (http://www.news-medical.net/health/Meditation-Spirituality-and-Religion.aspx). (Some contain elements that you can pick and choose from in order to find an option that works for you, even if you're not religious.)

People of the Baha'i faith recite an Arabic phrase meaning "God is most Glorious" 95 times. A non-religious alternative could be reciting affirmations that are meaningful to you.

Buddhist meditation focuses on transforming the mind through meditation. A non-religious application is to look at some of your unhealthy beliefs and spend focused time thinking about the opposite beliefs.

Christians often focus their meditations on Bible verses and think deeply about specific words and phrases. A non-religious alternative would be to think deeply on a quote that inspires or challenges you in some way.

If you think meditation is too "woo-woo" for serious business owners, consider a *Huffington Post* article (http://www.huffingtonpost.com/2013/07/05/business-meditation-executives-meditate_n_3528731.html) that showcases the impact meditation had in the lives of some of the most successful entrepreneurs—like Oprah Winfrey, Bill Ford (executive chairman of Ford Motor company) and Arianna Huffington (president and editor-in-chief of the Huffington Post Media Group). These people, along with other top entrepreneurs, have stated that meditation can help you:

- Reboot your brain and soul

- Quiet your busy mind
- Reduce pain issues (e.g., migraines)
- Develop positive attributes such as patience
- Fill yourself with hope, contentment and joy
- Increase creativity

Peaceful meditation is not only good for the soul—it can alsoimpact your bottom line because it disciplines your thinking.

Journaling

Maybe meditation isn't your thing, or perhaps you simply think better with a pen in your hand. Through journaling, not only will you be able to organize your thoughts, but you'll also develop a written record of your ideas so you can refer back to them in the future.

Journaling doesn't have to be complicated or particularly "deep." It's okay to do some stream-of-consciousness writing that has no real objective other than getting what is in your mind onto paper.

In *The Artist's Way* (http://www.developgoodhabits.com/artists-way), author Judith Cameron encourages the daily practice of what she refers to as "morning pages." During this exercise, you set a timer for 15 minutes and do some stream-of-consciousness writing until the timer goes off.

If you can't think of anything to write about, just write something like this: "This is dumb. I can't think of anything to write." At some point in the process, you will begin to write things that are beneath the surface of your mind and may be blocking you in some way. While Cameron insists that morning pages should be handwritten, Rebecca finds it easier to type them. Do whatever works best for you.

A key thing to keep in mind with journaling is that it doesn't have to be done a certain way. The best journaling rule is that there are no real rules. Just do it as consistently as possible.

IMPLEMENTATION

Developing a meditation (or journaling) habit isn't that hard to do. Here are a few actions for getting started:

Action 1: Choose to either journal or meditate on a daily basis. While there is value in doing both, you'll have more success if you start off with just the one that appeals to you the most.

Acton 2: Commit to journaling or meditating for just five to ten minutes a day at first. One book, *The Five Minute Journal: A Happier You in Five Minutes Per Day* (http://www.developgoodhabits.com/five-minute-journal), is obviously focused on producing maximum results in a short period of time each day. (Note: Many people find it helpful to do this either first thing in the morning or right before going to sleep at night.)

Action 3: If using a fancy journal inspires you to write, buy the fanciest one you can find. If you don't want to mess up a really nice journal, grab a cheap spiral notebook.

If you prefer to go high-tech, purchase an app such as the Five Minute Journal app (http://app.fiveminutejournal.com/), Day One (http://dayoneapp.com/) or Diaro (https://play.google.com/store/apps/details?id=com.pixelcrate r.Diaro&hl=en).

ESH #31: Do What You Love

As an entrepreneur, you may be hyper-focused on work. After all, if you aren't disciplined and don't work hard, you'll never make it in business. But as the old saying goes, "All work and no play makes Jack a dull boy."(In 1825, Irish novelist Maria Edgeworth said, "All play and no work makes Jack a mere toy.") (http://en.wikipedia.org/wiki/All_work_and_no_play_makes_Jack_a_dull_boy)

Indeed, a blend of work and play keeps many of us productive. By regularly doing things you enjoy, you can find that balance of being a successful entrepreneur while reducing stress and preventing burnout.

Artist Dates

For example, Judith Cameron writes in *The Artist's Way* about the importance of going on a weekly "artist date." Artist dates can help you refuel and keep the creativity flowing.

While artist dates have very few rules, the one rule—at least according to Judith Cameron—is that you need to do them alone, so they are not something you take a spouse, friend or child to. (Of course, you can decide whether or not to follow that rule.) The core benefit of doing things alone is that you don't have to worry about pleasing anyone else while on your artist date. That may sound selfish, but it really can make a difference when it comes to refueling.

You Don't Have to Be an Artist to Benefit from Artist Dates

An important thing to remember is that artist dates can benefit any entrepreneur, even if you don't consider yourself to be any type of artist.

Here are some ways that artist dates can benefit both artists and non-artists alike:

Benefit 1: They can help you see things from a different perspective. Regardless of your industry, you are bound to experience some challenges and uncertainties.

While you shouldn't intentionally think about your business while you're on an artist date, removing yourself from your business and doing something for fun may cause the solution to a problem to pop into your head.

Benefit 2: Artist dates are rejuvenating. Let's face it: Running a business is hard work. If you don't do things to relax and refuel, it can be easy to burn out.

Artist dates can help you temporarily forget about your business problems and relieve stress so that you'll be ready to jump back into your business with renewed energy and enthusiasm.

Benefit 3: You might meet someone who can help your business while out on an artist date. We've already stated that you should go on artist dates alone, but if you typically work in isolation, getting out of the house and meeting other people can do you good.

There's a lot you can do with an artist date. If you need some ideas, check out a post by *The Artist's Way Blog* for 101 ideas (http://theartistswayblog.wordpress.com/2010/10/17/101-artists-date-ideas/). That should be enough to get you started and to get the wheels turning for some artist dates that may work for you.

Beyond Artist Dates

Artist dates are just one way to add fun to your life. While artist dates are a solitary endeavor, some of the most enjoyable things in life are shared with others.

For example, you may want to do fun things with family members and friends. Ideas include a weekly game session, a night out with friends, watching a show or movie, or simply listening to music that pumps you up. The key is to incorporate fun and refreshing activities into your life on a regular basis.

IMPLEMENTATION

Recharging *outside* of work is important for your success as an entrepreneur. That's why it's important to do the following:

Action 1: Plan a weekly artist date to spend time alone doing something you enjoy that will refresh you. If that doesn't sound appealing, then schedule a fun activity that's shared with friends or family members. The key is to schedule it like any other important appointment on your calendar.

Action 2: Consider taking up a hobby that you've perhaps done in the past but have neglected since you started your business. It doesn't have to be a major time-consuming activity—just something that requires 15 to 30 minutes a day. That's enough to relax and unwind.

Action 3: Add small bits of enjoyment to each day, such as brewing a special type of tea or taking a walk in the park. Whenever you feel the pressures of business creeping up, take a quick break and enjoy a quick activity.

ESH #32: Help Others

As an entrepreneur, it's natural to focus on business-related goals. In fact, you can easily become so wrapped up in personal achievement that others who take up your time are an imposition. To balance things out, it's important to develop a habit of helping others. The amazing thing is, when you help others, you actually end up helping yourself as well.

For example, doing regular volunteer work can provide you with the following benefits:

- You'll improve your social and relationship skills—especially if you are shy and find it difficult to initiate conversations with people.
- You'll be less depressed. One cause of depression is isolation, so getting out among others is good for your mental health.
- You'll have an opportunity to escape from your normal, day-to-day activities. The change of pace can be a good break for you and give you an opportunity to experience something very different from your normal routine.
- You'll meet people you wouldn't otherwise meet. This can be a source of friendship, business contacts or other types of connections that may be helpful in the future.
- Your self-confidence will increase since it feels really good to help others.
- Volunteering can give you new knowledge or skills to apply to your own business.

Furthermore, according to this *Huffington Post* article (http://www.huffingtonpost.com/2013/12/28/health-benefits-of-helping-others_n_4427697.html), there are four health benefits to helping others:

Benefit 1: Volunteering can add years to your life. Volunteers see a 20 percent reduction in mortality compared to those who don't volunteer.

Benefit 2: Acts of kindness can result in what some refer to as a "helper's high." A study found that those who participated in five acts of kindness one day a week for six weeks experienced a boost in overall feelings of well-being.

Interestingly enough, those who spread their acts of goodwill throughout the week didn't experience the same benefit, which indicates that having more concentrated times of helping others yields bigger results when it comes to the "feel good" aspect of volunteering.

Benefit 3: Helping others who have problems similar to yours can help you overcome your own problems. For example, helping those who have chronic pain issues can actually reduce the amount of pain you experience if you also deal with chronic pain.

Benefit 4: Being kind to others can lower your blood pressure. People age 50 and over who volunteer at least two hundred hours over the course of a year (approximately four hours per week) are forty percent less likely to have high blood pressure than people in the same age group who don't volunteer.

Where to Find Volunteer Opportunities

You don't need to look for official opportunities if you want to randomly help people. Simply keep your eyes peeled for positive things to do on a regular basis. For instance, if you see a mom who is having a hard time opening a door while pushing a stroller, jump in and help. The idea here is to practice *random acts of kindness* and look for ways to do little things for strangers.

If you prefer something more structured, join organizations that focus on volunteer opportunities. Here are some places to get started:

- Places of worship such as synagogues and churches
- Youth organizations such as Boy Scouts, Girl Scouts and after-school programs
- Libraries
- Pet rescue organizations and animal shelters
- National parks
- Community gardens
- Rescue missions and homeless shelters
- Organizations such as the Rotary Club and Lions Club
- Historical venues such as monuments, historic homes and museums
- Community theaters

Before agreeing to volunteer, make sure the position is right for you. The values of the organization should align with yours, it should be work that you'll enjoy and the opportunity should fit in well with your other responsibilities.

IMPLEMENTATION

Helping others can be a powerful habit that not only improves your personal life, but also enhances the enjoyment of your business. The following are two actions for turning this information into a daily routine.

Action 1: Choose one day a week where you'll focus on helping others. This could be something as simple as writing thank you notes to people every Thursday (e.g., "Thankful Thursday"), volunteering in a soup kitchen once a week or simply going out of your way to open doors for people or buy coffee for strangers one day a week.

Action 2: Also, create a habit where you help one single person every single day. Start with the people closest to you: your family, friends, neighbors and colleagues.

You could also practice one random act of kindness every single day. Find more information about this idea by checking out The Random Acts of Kindness Foundation's website (http://www.randomactsofkindness.org/).

Finally, don't get caught up in doing big things. Small things make a difference as well. As Mother Teresa said, "Not all of us can do great things. But we can do small things with great love."

ESH #33: Believe in Yourself

It's hard to be successful when you don't believe in yourself. Without self-confidence, you're less likely to try new things, take risks or even find that next client. Bottom line—if you don't believe in yourself, it will be hard for *other people* to have confidence in your abilities.

Rebecca and Steve have both suffered from what is known as impostor syndrome (http://en.wikipedia.org/wiki/Impostor_syndrome). People who suffer from this syndrome believe they're frauds and, in spite of evidence to the contrary, feel they don't deserve the success they've achieved. They often feel like their "cover will be blown" and people will find out the truth that their success is based on luck.

The authors are not alone in this feeling. According to psychological research done in the 1980s, approximately 70 percent of people feel like frauds at least some of the time. Grad students, high-achieving females and African Americans are most likely to have this problem, but it can be experienced by others who don't fit into those categories. One example is bestselling author Neil Gaiman, a Caucasian male.

The fact that high achievers experience this indicates that you can *still* be successful despite suffering from impostor syndrome. However, it's harder to enjoy the success since you feel like you don't truly deserve it.

Impostor syndrome or not, many entrepreneurs feel inadequate. To take your business to the next level, you need to implement strategies for overcoming these negative thought patterns.

Get Positive Support from Others

The simplest way to overcome imposter syndrome is to surround yourself with people who believe in you. The goal here is to get regular encouragement and a genuine pat on the back for a job well done. This type of support from those who know you well can help you to truly believe that you have something unique to offer to the world.

For example, while Rebecca still struggles with impostor syndrome, she has largely overcome it as a result of a very supportive husband who constantly affirms her and tells her how amazing she is. He asks her things such as, "Do you think all the people who say good things about you are wrong?" This helps her think about herself more objectively.

Additionally, you should spend less time around people who tear you down. You may not be able to avoid negative people completely, especially if they're family members, but try hard to reduce the amount of time you spend with them.

You Have Something Special to Offer to the World

We all have gifts to share with the world. It's important to not just use them for your own gain, but also to enrich other people's lives. Now is the time to silence your inner critic, live life to the fullest and be all that you were meant to be.

IMPLEMENTATION

We all have moments of doubt, so it's silly to think you'll go through an entire day with a Stepford Wife grin plastered on your face. Instead, you need to have a strategy to improve your mood when you're feeling those moments of self-doubt. Here's how to do this:

Action 1: Keep a file of positive things people say about you. For instance, if you get an email praising you, add it to the file. Ask your customers for testimonials and add them to this ever-growing file. Read through it whenever you feel insecure.

Action 2: Choose your friends and associates wisely, and avoid those who have a tendency to tear you down. Don't compare yourself with others. Instead, compare your current self with your past self, and always strive to make improvements.

Action 3: Send an email to 25 of the people who know you best, asking them to describe your three most positive traits. Add all of the responses to your "positive things about me" file. (And don't take it personally if only a small number respond. That's normal.)

Action 4: Write a list of your strong points. Repeat them as affirmations on a regular basis.

Action 5: Set realistic expectations regarding your goals. If you set goals that are so high they're impossible to reach, you'll beat yourself up—no matter what you've accomplished.

Overall, it's important to expect failure in both business and life. It doesn't make you a failure or an imposter. Just remember that when you fail, your #1 priority is to get back up and try again.

Conclusion

We've now covered 33 habits that can improve your success as an entrepreneur. At this point, you have a lot of different options. So you might wonder, *"Where do I start?"*

Well, we recommend that you do the following to take action on this information.

First, think of the biggest obstacle you're currently experiencing with your business. This will be one of the five challenges we discussed at the beginning of the book:

1. Failing to Achieve Professional Goals
2. Not Getting Things Done
3. Increasing Competition
4. Poor Business Relationships
5. Stress and Burnout

We all have different things that hold us back from achieving our best. Your job is to spend time considering what troubles you on a daily basis. Is there something that keeps you awake at night and fills your mind with anxiety? If so, that's the best place to start.

Next, review the section related to that challenge. Check out the different options (i.e. habits) that *could* resolve that particular issue. Odds are, doing one of these habits on a regular basis can help you overcome this challenge.

Some will require a complete shift in your daily routine, while others might only take a few minutes each day to complete. Our advice is to start with the "small win" actions and build from there.

What you pick is entirely up to you, but you want to focus on the actions that will have an immediate impact on your business.

Third, complete the nine-step process for turning this action into a permanent, lifelong habit:

1. Focus on one habit at a time while ignoring any distractions.
2. Add it to a habit-stacking routine if it takes less than five minutes to complete.
3. Commit to the habit for the next 30 days.
4. Anchor the new habit to an established, reliable routine.
5. Take baby steps by committing to a small outcome and improving on it.
6. Create accountability through social media and apps.
7. Overcome setbacks with an if-then plan.
8. Celebrate important milestones by doing simple, fun activities.
9. Build a new identity that makes this habit part of who you are.

Finally, I urge you to learn all you can from each new habit. Keep the ones that make sense for your business, then toss out the rest.

You'll find that what you do on a daily basis often changes from week to week. This is a natural part of the success process. You'll find that you evolve as the business evolves, increasing your personal satisfaction and putting you on the road to success.

We wish you the best of luck.

Steve "S.J." Scott

http://www.DevelopGoodHabits.com

Rebecca Livermore

http://www.ProfessionalContentCreation.com/

Would You Like To Know More?

You can learn a lot more about habit development in Steve's other Kindle books. The best part? He frequently runs special promotions where he offers free or discounted books (usually $0.99) on Amazon.

One way to get instant notifications for these deals is to subscribe to Steve's email list. By joining not only will you receive updates on the latest offer, you'll also get a free copy of his book "77 Good Habits to Live a Better Life."

Check out the below link to learn more.

http://www.developgoodhabits.com/free-updates

Did You Like "The Daily Entrepreneur?"

Before you go, we'd like to say "thank you" for purchasing our book.

You could have picked from dozens of books on habit development, but you took a chance to check out this one.

So a big thanks for downloading this book and reading all the way to the end.

Now we'd like ask for a *small* favor. **Could you please take a minute or two and leave a review for this book on Amazon**.

This feedback will help us continue to write the kind of Kindle books that help you get results. And if you loved it, then please let me know :-)

39294876R00094

Made in the USA
Lexington, KY
15 February 2015